MAYWOOD PUBLIC LIBRARY

W9-BUH-340

Maywood Public Library
121 S. 5th Ave.
Maywood, IL 60153

Trolley Car Treasury

Frank Rowsome, Jr.

Technical Editor, Stephen D. Maguire

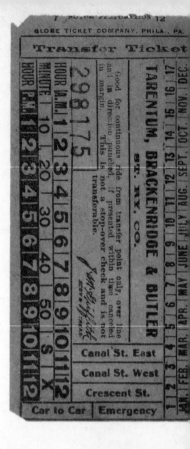

7   [illegible]   12
GLOBE TICKET COMPANY, PHILA. PA.
Transfer Ticket
298175
Good for continuous ride from transfer point only,
and in direction punched, if presented within time canceled
in margin. This is not a stop-over check and is not
transferable.
TARENTUM, BRACKENRIDGE & BUTLER
ST. RY. CO.
HOUR (A.M.) 1 2 3 4 5 6 7 8 9 10 11 12
MINUTE   10 20 30 40 50 S X
HOUR (P.M.) 1 2 3 4 5 6 7 8 9 10 11 12
Canal St. East
Canal St. West
Crescent St.
Car to Car   Emergency

TROLLEY CAR

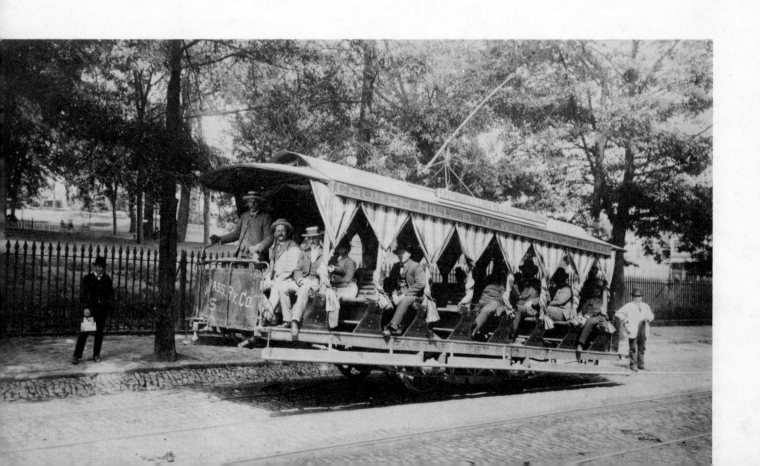

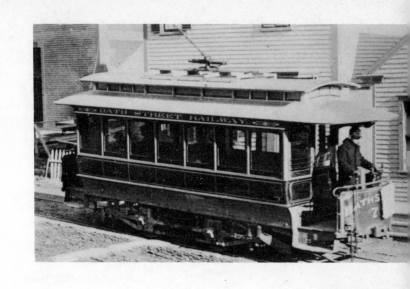

TREASURY

A Century of American Streetcars—
Horsecars, Cable Cars, Interurbans,
and Trolleys

BONANZA BOOKS · NEW YORK

This edition published by Bonanza Books, a division of
Crown Publishers, Inc., by arrangement with
the McGraw-Hill Book Company, Inc.

TROLLEY CAR TREASURY. Copyright © 1956 by Frank
Rowsome, Jr., and Stephen D. Maguire. All rights in
this book are reserved. It may not be used for dramatic,
motion-, or talking-picture purposes without written
authorization from the holder of these rights. Nor may
the book or parts thereof be reproduced in any manner
whatsoever without permission in writing, except in the
case of brief quotations embodied in critical articles
and reviews. For information, address the McGraw-Hill
Book Company, Inc., Trade Department, 330 West 42d
Street, New York 36, New York.

Library of Congress Catalog Card Number: 56–11054

DESIGN BY JOSEPH J. BINNS

Published by the McGraw-Hill Book Company, Inc.
Printed in the United States of America

To

tireless inventors, able superintendents,

conductors and motormen by the thousands,

trolley fans and historians,

and hardworking horses

like Maud and Old Crooked Tail,

this book is admiringly dedicated.

Acknowledgments

Many have contributed to this book: professional and amateur historians, present and past traction-company men, several railway historical societies, librarians and researchers, magazine editors and photographers, and literally scores of streetcar enthusiasts. The writer has had the benefit of continuous guidance from Stephen D. Maguire as well as access to his immense collection of streetcar material, which is probably the largest private collection of its sort in the world. Another invaluable source of both information and perspective has been Felix E. Reifschneider, who has been unfailingly helpful.

E. J. Quinby, of the E.R.A. and the Branford group, supplied much valuable material and good counsel. Harriet Sprague was a courteous source of information about her husband's career. Published material by John A. Miller, Vincent F. Seyfried, Lucius Beebee and Charles Clegg, Ira Swett, Robert Wilson, and Richard Steinmetz provided many specific details. Research for little-known details on the earliest cars was done by Terry Robbins and Trudy Ray. Many good suggestions were supplied by George Walrath, Herbert Summers, Al Cramer, Blair Foulds, and George Krambles.

The editor of *The Model Engineer,* London, provided a rare view of the sea-going trolley. Special thanks are owed to Freeman Hubbard, editor of *Railroad Magazine;* to the American Transit Association; and to the following individuals for many pictures: J. William Barnes, G. Barrett, J. O. Brew, Donald T. Bimes, George Bindley, Roger Borrup, Fielding L. Bowman, Theodore Santarelli de Brasch, C. A. Brown, Kent W. Cochrane, Randall Comfort, Wilbourne B. Cox, H. T. Crittenden, O. R. Cummings, A. F. Day, Theodore C. Day, G. A. Doeright, G. R. Eggers, Alexander Faubert, J. Felix, Edward T. Francis, W. J. B. Gwinn, Grahame Hardy, A. E. Hickerson, H. Hinrichs, R. Donaldson Horton, John Hughes, Donald Idarius, W. C. Janssen, W. E. Johns, Dick Johnson, John H. Keller, Leroy O. King, Michael L. Lavelle, Albert Lohmann, Jr., W. A. Lucas, K. S. MacDonald, John Woods Marchildon, A. Andrew Merrilees, Edward H. Meyers, R. P. Middlebrook, Howard Moulton, Sen. Richard Neuberger, Barney Neuburger, Everett Ortner, F. D. Pangborn, W. C. Persons, C. C. Pierce, John H. Powers, J. H. Richards, John F. Robinson, B. A. Schwartz, J. R. Slevin, L. S. Slevin, Donald K. Slick, C. L. Smith, John Gibb Smith, Jr., H. S. Thorne, Vitaly Y. Uzoff, Lorin E. Vail, George E. Votava, Lewis C. Wilcox, Lester K. Wismer, and Richard H. Young.

Contents

1. DON'T TALK TO THE MOTORMAN

I am coming, I am coming, hark you hear my motor humming,
For the trolley's come to conquer, so you cannot keep it back;
And Zip! the sparks are flashing, as the car goes onward dashing
While the wheels are whirring smoothly along a perfect track.

—From "The Song of the Trolley"

No one, not knowing, would be likely to guess from the few docile vehicles running today the vigor and importance that streetcars have had in the recent American past. They have gone from among us with dismaying speed, like our youth, and the memory of their past vitality grows dimmer each year. Today trolleys run in only a handful of cities, and they are mostly a uniform, sterile sort, lacking the gritty and eccentric demeanor of their predecessors. It would be extremely difficult to recall the present rubbery vehicles with sentiment; it would be hard to think of the wonderful old trolleys—the bouncy little single-truck cars, the great center-door mammoths, and the breezy open cars—without affection.

Still rarer today are the interurbans. Only a few lines survive, with scarcely a trace of their kingly status of forty-five years ago. In their time of power and glory the great interurban lines were stealing ever-increasing revenue from the steam railroads, and their future shone bright. Especially to youngsters was the interurban an awesome thing. Each big electric car rumbled arrogantly through the city streets out to its private right-of-way with the suppressed power of a destroyer easing through a harbor of fishing boats. Once in the country it raced through the fields with a hiss to the trolley wire, its great arc headlight drilling the dusk and its big flaring cowcatcher grimacing dangerously. As it swept past you there was the beat of the air compressor and a glimpse of plushy comforts, perhaps arched windows topped by stained glass as an ultimate luxury. When it had rocked by and was gone with a diminishing hiss overhead, there on the rails were the two crossed nails you had left to be flattened, welded together as a souvenir of the glory you had seen.

Buried deeper in the American memory are the curious and often touching cars that came before the great days. There were the first shaky electrics, as advanced and disquieting in their day as atomic reactors in ours. Before them were the cable cars that now survive only as a nurtured tourist attraction. There were the valiant, slightly cockeyed first efforts to bring mechanical power to street transportation—odd vehicles propelled by compressed air, ammonia, steam, and giant clock springs. And before them all were the horsecars, now merely a quaint image but in their time a bustling and prosperous network that changed the shape of cities and the habits of their dwellers.

For all their proliferation and vitality, this army of old streetcars has almost entirely vanished. The survivors are fewer each year, and soon they too will be gone. They won't be back.

No one man invented the trolley, in the sense that Morse, say, can be credited with the telegraph. Instead, scores of inventors independently had the bright dream of electric transportation—long before there were useful motors or adequately powerful sources of electricity. For decades these men built cars that were certain to fail, not so much because they were imperfect inventors, but simply and sadly because they had dreamed too soon.

Even before the Civil War a few visionaries were at work. The task was hopeless then: motors were curiosities, scarcely better than toys, and only meager amounts of electricity could be coaxed from fragile wet-cell batteries. By the mid-seventies motors and dynamos of marginal usefulness appeared, but the practical problem of developing something that could compete with horse and cable cars was still enormous. It is one thing to devise a mechanism that will behave itself in a sheltered world where its inventor can shower it with loving attentions, and quite another to build something that can survive in the everyday world of mud, rain, bankers, and abuse.

In half a dozen American cities in the mid-eighties electric streetcars made halting debuts. Each was hailed as a marvel of science and a distinguished cause for local pride; and each expired after the frustrations of irregular service, burned-out equipment, and incessant derailment. Horses were generally called back on the job for a few years. Then in 1888 a young Annapolis graduate named Frank Sprague turned the trick. In Richmond, Virginia, he built an ambitious 12-mile, forty-car line that, despite nightmarish difficulties, managed to keep running. Both its size and survival were unprecedented, and it quickly attracted the attention of horsecar officials all over the country. Soon scores of similar lines were abuilding.

Rebuilt from horsecars, the earliest electrics were

Striped awning on the Oregon Electric's observation car caused open-mouthed wonderment in youngsters at the trackside.

When the weather was pleasant, the grip car was preferable to a closed trailer car. San Francisco in 1883.

A standard horsecar in Oakland, Calif., in 1880. The impish lad at left above grew up to be the city's chief of police.

For those on farms or in hamlets, the interurbans brought exciting new scope and freedom. This one ran in central Maine.

Two men and two mustaches crewed this West Virginia open car about 1889. With no pole, it used a Daft "troller."

The first really successful trolleys were Sprague's cars in Richmond, Va. This one was an improved model.

One of Sprague's original Richmond cars. A counterweight and two coil springs pulled the trolley pole upwards.

uncertain craft. On some the motor was mounted on the front platform, so that nothing was more natural than to christen the electrician standing bravely beside it a "motorman." But since flimsy horsecar platforms showed a tendency to shake to pieces under this load, the motor was soon moved down near the wheels. Speeds were low, perhaps eight or nine miles an hour when all went well.

All rarely did, at first. The open, unshielded motors sparked furiously, something that not only alarmed timid passengers but also necessitated endless repairs. The controller—the speed-governing device under the motorman's left hand—was jerky at best and prone to catch fire at worst. (Aggrieved firemen discovered, moreover, that when a hose was directed upon an electrical fire, electrical current could come back up the stream even faster than water came out the nozzle and knock them on their backs.) Brakes, borrowed unchanged from horsecars, were mute testimony to how much of the total braking effort had been contributed by a well-trained team of horses. Early electric-car brakes mildly discouraged movement so long as the motorman kept the slack wound up and had a brawny right arm. The intricate problem of feeding electricity to a moving car, in two polarities that could only be allowed to meet in the motor, was a poser to early designers. Inevitably, some lines tried the obvious: positive electricity in one rail and negative in the other. But switches and mud puddles brought complications, and the discovery that a pedestrian or horse touching both rails at once would become wildly exhilarated made further difficulties.

A man named Daft invented a system employing two overhead wires, strung side by side, on which there ran a toy-sized cart or dolly. Flexible wires dangled from the dolly to the car beneath, which towed—trolled—it along like a child dragging a roller skate on a string. It was variously called a "troller" or "trolley"—the latter a term for any wheeled object running on wire. The Daft system proved very troublesome: the troller kept falling off the wire and landing with a terrifying crash on the car roof. Daft cars tended in consequence to be so leaky that in heavy rains passengers usually kept their umbrellas raised inside.

In the early days even the protective devices could be alarming. Crude fuses were often used to save the motors from overload damage—exposed strips of thin wire designed to burn out just before the motor would. The difficulty was that these "ribbon" fuses could let go with a brilliant yellow flash and a deafening report, a stimulus that on several occasions sent taut passengers right out through the windows. After several blown-fuse panics had brought injury and lawsuits, the early lines took to shielding their fuses so that the stimulus wouldn't be so overpowering.

The troubles weren't all technical. In 1889 a new trolley line in Seattle was sued for damages. The plaintiff, a woman, testified that she had been lying abed in a rooming house as one of the strange new cars had clanked by outside. Simultaneously she had received a severe shock, causing great personal anguish. "I saw the electricity," she stated, "attack me from the ceiling." In its defense the company produced experts who testified that such a shock was an impossibility. It was tactfully suggested that what she might have seen was the reflection on the white ceiling of a flash outside. The jury, though cognizant that much of electricity was a freakish mystery, found for the trolley company and withheld damages.

This particular anguished lady may well have been influenced by the sharp public disputes—by no means limited to Seattle—that preceded the granting of many early trolley franchises. In the beginning, cable and horse lines were fiercely opposed to the "cars run by lightning," and in this they were usually joined by the solid, property-owning citizens who disapproved, in principle, of radical new ideas. Word got around of how trolleys "forced electricity into the ground," subjecting water pipes to a destructive corrosion called electrolysis. It was widely rumored that the blue sparks flashing from trolley poles were injurious to eyesight. Everyone knew how telephones could become worthless whenever a trolley was running nearby and how during storms the overhead wires invited thunderbolts that could easily incinerate foolhardy riders. An attorney for a cable-car company once wound up his speech of opposition against a trolley franchise with these words:

Steadiness in the running of street cars is essential; electricity is shocking and eccentric. Its shocks will make the cars jump off the tracks and endanger the lives of passengers. Water is a conductor and rain will divert the electric current from the wires, leaving the cars dead on the tracks or dependent on the brakes to hold them if on a grade. Collisions and appalling accidents will inevitably occur.

Such telling opposition might have held back the trolley for years, except for the fact that many horse and cable companies, eyeing the cost advantages of electric cars, jumped into the business themselves. As it was, some timidity marked public attitudes for a short time. There was a noticeable air of bravado about the first trolley riders. Men would hand their pocket watches to their stay-behind womenfolk be-

Minneapolis had electric cars in 1886. They ran erratically.

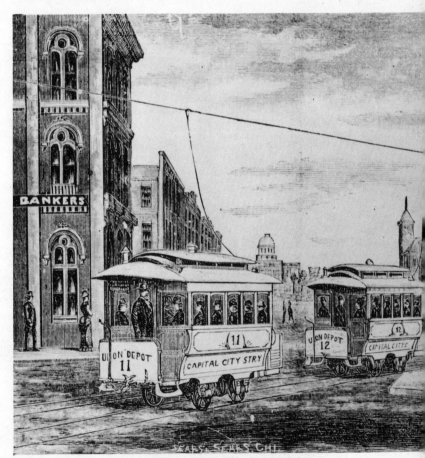

By 1886 electric cars also ran in Montgomery, Ala., but incessant failures plagued the little streetcar system.

The last word in breezy electrics in 1892. A trolley pole bent this way could mean that the car had been backed carelessly.

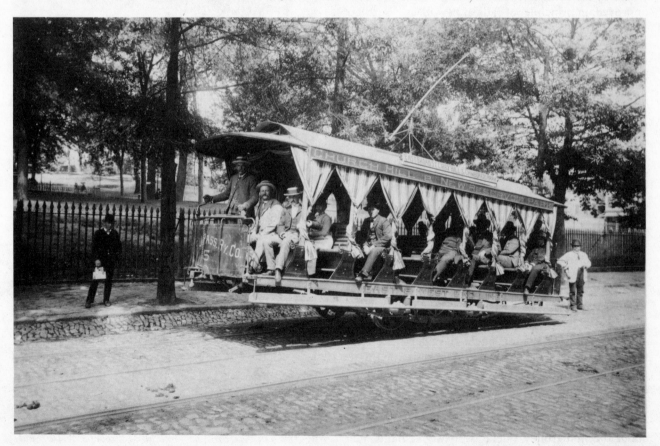

A hose jumper—a tiny steel bridge placed on the rails to allow fire hoses to cross the tracks—made this car tilt back.

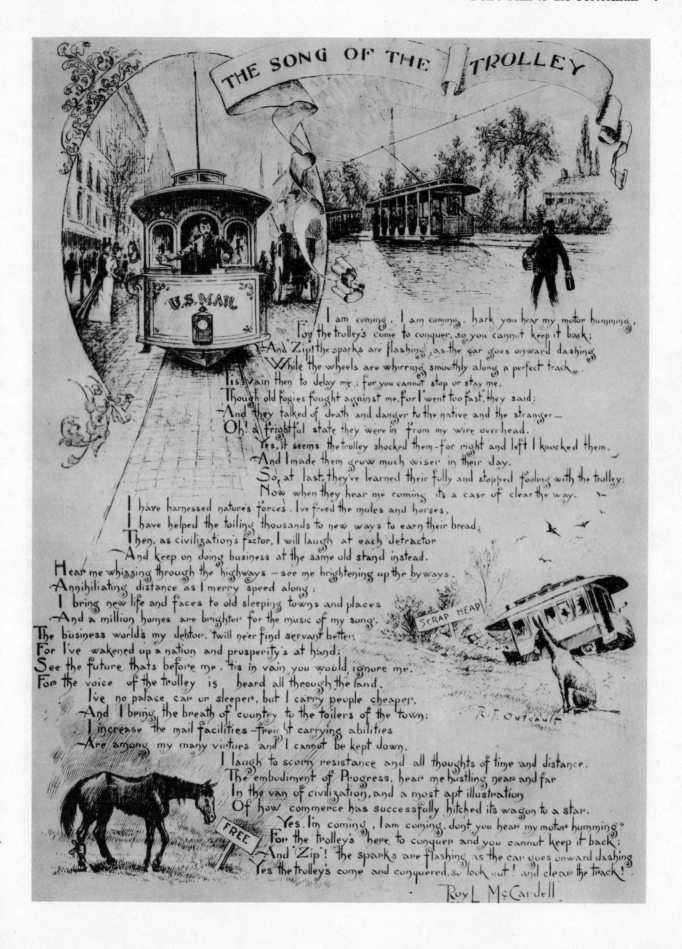

THE SONG OF THE TROLLEY

I am coming, I am coming, hark you hear my motor humming,
For the trolley's come to conquer, so you cannot keep it back;
And "Zip!" the sparks are flashing, as the car goes onward dashing
While the wheels are whirring smoothly along a perfect track.
'Tis vain then to delay me, for you cannot stop or stay me,
Though old fogies fought against me, for I went too fast, they said;
And they talked of death and danger to the native and the stranger—
Oh! a frightful state they were in from my wire overhead.
Yes, it seems the trolley shocked them—for right and left I knocked them,
And I made them grow much wiser in their day.
So, at last, they've learned their folly and stopped fooling with the trolley;
Now when they hear me coming it's a case of clear the way.
I have harnessed nature's forces, I've freed the mules and horses,
I have helped the toiling thousands to new ways to earn their bread;
Then, as civilization's factor, I will laugh at each detractor
And keep on doing business at the same old stand instead.
Hear me whizzing through the highways—see me brightening up the byways,
Annihilating distance as I merry speed along;
I bring new life and faces to old sleeping towns and places
And a million homes are brighter for the music of my song.
The business world's my debtor, 'twill ne'er find servant better,
For I've wakened up a nation and prosperity's at hand;
See the future thats before me, 'tis in vain you would ignore me,
For the voice of the trolley is heard all through the land.
I've no palace car or sleeper, but I carry people cheaper,
And I bring the breath of country to the toilers of the town;
I increase the mail facilities—freight carrying abilities
Are among my many virtues and I cannot be kept down.
I laugh to scorn resistance and all thoughts of time and distance.
The embodiment of Progress, hear me hustling near and far
In the van of civilization, and a most apt illustration
Of how commerce has successfully hitched its wagon to a star.
Yes, I'm coming, I am coming, dont you hear my motor humming?
For the trolley's here to conquer and you cannot keep it back;
And "Zip"! the sparks are flashing as the car goes onward dashing
Yes the trolley's come and conquered, so look out! and clear the track!

Roy L. McCardell

R.T. Outcault

cause the powerful electric currents flowing invisibly about a car might magnetize them. Some riders joked elaborately about how in 1888 New York State had decided that electrocution was a fitting way to dispose of murderers. It was held prudent to debark hastily if a thunderstorm sprang up; on some lines it was a regular practice to stop and pull down trolley poles whenever thunder rumbled nearby.

But there was counterpropaganda from trolley companies. When one of the earliest lines in the country was opened in Montgomery, Alabama, the local *Advertiser* reported:

Some people think that in the electric-motor system for street railways there is a possibility of danger to passengers. "It is all a mistake," said a practical electrician to an *Advertiser* reporter. "In fact there can be

no danger in the electric-motor system. You might receive the entire current of electricity that will operate the cars and the shock would be comparatively light. There is really less danger than there is in steam power. If a car should jump the track no harm could result because the motive power ceases the moment the wheels leave the rails. There is more real danger, ten to one, in a Texas mule's heels than in all the electric-motor system."

Company propaganda wasn't needed for long. Americans speedily took the new trolleys to their hearts, riding them with a regularity that soon made streetcars a basic part of life in the United States. In just a few years a wonderful golden age began for the trolley, to continue until the First World War. Open cars had their flowering—breezy, slatting vehicles that on sweltering summer evenings meant blessed

On the way to the Hambletonian trotting race at Goshen, N.Y., a loaded open car meets a returning one on a passing track.

The front seat of an open car was a fine place to ride on a sweltering summer afternoon. Taken in 1907 at Troy, N.Y.

coolness and escape in that non-air-conditioned era. It was a time, too, when trolley financiers had visions of wealth beyond avarice, when traction companies stirred in a turmoil of expansion, and when trolley bonds were the gilt-edged favorites in the portfolios of the prosperous. It was then that interurbans developed into a threatening competitor of steam railroads, offering fast, low-cost transportation complete with parlor cars and diners. And it was then that many a trolley company, bursting with energy, jumped into such diverse activities as promoting real estate and cemeteries, renting out special cars for weddings and funerals, and operating picnic parks, vaudeville theaters, and zoos.

Trolleying out to Electric Park on a Saturday afternoon was an experience for which there is no exact equivalent today. Although the car might be similar to the one taken every day to work or school, its atmosphere was entirely different: you were all traveling together on a pleasure trip, to a place owned by the traction company and run for the purpose of entertaining you. The people aboard—young couples, large families with small babies, decorous but aware members of the opposite sex—reflected a mood wholly different from that of workaday riders. Everyone was trigged out in Saturday-at-the-park clothes,

including freshly ironed peekaboo shirtwaists, bird-trimmed hats, and, on the mustached young men, stripes and derbies or bright-ribboned sailor straws. People were laden with the impedimenta of a day off: sandwiches and deviled eggs in a shoebox, bathing suits, water wings, Brownie cameras, lap robes, extra diapers, sand pails and shovels, fielder's mitts, and very likely a mandolin—the latter in case the occasion arose in a canoe for any choruses of "Good-bye, Dolly Gray," "In the Good Old Summertime," or "The End of a Perfect Day."

Gliding along past the outskirts of town, the streetcar would finally swing in under the arched entrance to Electric Park. There the riders debarked to saunter along the flower-lined walks where tame peacocks strutted on the grass and the exciting Ferris wheel or giant aerial swings could be glimpsed beyond the trees. From the moment a person stepped off the trolley he'd hear the merry-go-round calliope, or the Sousaphone and drums from the bandstand, or the click and roar of the roller coaster and the screams from its ecstatically terrified riders. Hours later, when day was done and the trolley carried its load back to the city, there was still a feeling of pleasantly fatigued gaiety within the car. Despite the sunburn and blisters, the frankfurters and taffy lying leaden in the belly, the querulous baby with sand in its creases, the collective mood would be voiced by

A Toronto open car of the nineties. A moonlight ride around the city on warm nights was very popular.

Squeezed between two streetcars, a trick flivver draped with Keystone cops could shake movie-theater rafters.

the group in the back of the car that experimented in harmonies for "By the Light of the Silvery Moon" and "The Rosary."

This was a Saturday way of life that passed on with the trolley.

Scarcely more than a decade after the first cautious riders were coaxed aboard the infant sparkers, trolleys had grown to be a national institution, beloved and indispensable. In buying a new house you gave thought to whether it was within easy walking distance of a trolley line; in investing in real estate you prayed that a new line would be laid close by, doubling the land's value. And it was repeatedly said, in explaining why trolley securities had a reliable yield that commended them to widows and orphans, "Well, people will *always* have to ride, won't they?"

Streetcar accidents have ranged all the way from the terrible to the ridiculous. Many a minor mishap and some serious ones resulted from a fact that everyone knew and then forgot: a streetcar was the only object that moved along roads that couldn't swerve aside to avoid trouble. Unfortunate vehicles that managed to get wedged between two trolleys going in opposite directions sometimes dramatized this unswervable trait. Occasionally it seemed that trolleys were so big and ponderous that they could cause accidents just by frightening people. Many a horse-

drawn wagon, swinging sharply to get out of the way of an approaching car, would catch its metalshod wheels in the rails and tip ludicrously over, all without being touched.

Fatal streetcar accidents commonly fell into two typical patterns: the rare high-speed derailment or collision, with characteristics resembling steam-railroad crashes, and the far commoner street-scene fatality, when some luckless person was caught unaware on the tracks. Neither was frequent, in terms of statistical exposure, but both produced some grimly memorable scenes.

The worst trolley catastrophe in the early days happened on a beautiful day in May, 1896, when the Canadian city of Victoria was celebrating its namesake Queen's birthday. There was to be a sham naval battle offshore and thousands jammed the trolleys to ride out to vantage points. One ill-starred little car, packed to suffocation with what is believed to have been 124 people, broke through some rotted timbers on the Point Ellice Bridge and plunged into the bay. There were 54 bodies recovered. But this was not the worst single trolley accident in history. In 1953, on a single-track line near Mexico City, two crowded cars met on a grade with lethal velocity, and 79 people were killed outright.

Such shockers have been rare in trolley history; even the worst wrecks on fast interurbans were not as catastrophic. From the beginning, individual pedestrians were most often the victims in trolley fatalities. In 1902, according to a government report, 831 pedestrians were killed in the United States by streetcars, compared with 265 passengers and 122 employees of traction companies. Though the figures seem shocking in the pre-auto era, they were small in

It wasn't always a joke. In the turmoils of early traffic, an errant auto sometimes got in a jam. New York, in 1925.

This trolley was literally shipwrecked in Milwaukee in 1905. A freighter crashed into one end of a drawbridge at the moment the car was leaving the other end.

terms of traffic; 1902 was a year in which American trolleys carried 5.8 *billion* riders. Still much inventive effort went into various pedestrian-protecting devices, notably fenders, which were bedspringlike contrivances on the front of cars, and life guards, shielding mechanisms in front of the wheels. They worked, but only after a fashion. When in the early years of the century the stem-winder hand brake was supplanted by air brakes, the greatest single step toward safety was taken. A Massachusetts investigating commission, after studying 104 patented fenders, commented with asperity that "the importance of fenders is insignificant compared to that of fitting cars with power brakes, in order to stop before striking an unfortunate individual, instead of trying to scoop him up after he has been struck." Air brakes or not, the commonest form of trolley accident was the rear-end collision. The combination of wet or greasy rails and heavy traffic was a trap for careless motormen. In the twenties instructor-motormen liked to recount the tale to their pupils of an earnest young motorman with an unblemished safety record. He was running in dense traffic in Newark, New Jersey, one day when an automobile close ahead stopped short. Full emergency brakes weren't enough, so the motorman slapped the controller into reverse and spun the wheels backward, dumping sand on the rails as he did so. It wasn't quite enough—his car slipped slowly into the rear of the sedan with a crunch and a tinkle, accordion-pleating its trunk. No one was injured, though the auto had to be towed away. Heartsick over the first accident on his clean slate, the earnest

young motorman did his prescribed paperwork, collecting the names and addresses of five witnesses. Then he inspected the undamaged front of his trolley, got back in, released the brake, and started up—to crunch sickeningly into an automobile immediately behind. He had left the controller in reverse.

Trolley cars have always shown a remarkable capacity to generate emotion. Sometimes, of course, the emotion was hostility. Teamsters never liked streetcars a bit. They took pleasure in arranging their drays during loading so as either to block the track completely or to compel a motorman to inch past, checking his clearance from the door. A Pennsylvania traction company once tried "the friendly gift of horse-blanket pins to every drayman in town, with a view to winning good will and lessening blockages." A large number of giant safety pins were disposed of, though no beneficial results could be detected, except perhaps to the comfort of horses. Motormen and teamsters grew to be traditional enemies and may have enjoyed the tradition. Each accused the other of blocking the streets needlessly and of having no regard for the rights of others. Years later, something of the teamsters' viewpoint came to be felt by motorists who disliked sharing the streets with such bulky, sluggish, and undentable things as trolleys.

Public hostility was also often the lot of streetcar companies as such. In the great days they were widely

Moseying riverward after it derailed, this Maine car carried 30 passengers to the brink. They debarked unhurt but uneasy. Splitting a switch was one frequent cause of derailment.

Posed fender demonstration. If the derbied motorman would forget the camera, he'd find a tyke on the fender.

A combined open and closed trolley, called a "California car," under New York's Third Ave. El in its steam days.

In 1940, on the last day that this Wilkes-Barre line operated, No. 356 munched up a sedan in a wholly malevolent fashion.

suspected of being excessively profitable, at least for their traction-baron manipulators. They were also generally believed to be in corrupt cahoots with city officials. It was held that uncomfortable rush-hour crowding and sluggish service weren't really necessary; it was just that the company was too stupid and avaricious to do better. Most streetcar companies, knowing little about the subtle arts of presenting a cosmetic face to the public gaze, suddenly discovered when hard times were upon them that they had become pariahs for whose bankruptcy no tears would be shed.

The commonest emotion that trolleys created, nevertheless, was a genuine affection. Maybe nobody liked the company but almost everybody was fond of the familiar cars, or of a genial conductor, or of one especially attractive trip. In every city countless people took trolley rides just for fun. Trolleys were a pleasant way by which to explore unknown parts of a

Riding an "electric" seemed fast and convenient in 1910. This N.J. streetcar added a touch of stylish dignity as well.

Packed with people dressed to the nines, an Elmira car with a double-decked trailer poses near Eldridge Park—1902.

An ultimate in open cars, this curious trolley long carried tourists for sightseeing rides around the city of Montreal.

city—they were leisurely and cheap and afforded a fine car-window view of the neighborhoods through which they passed. Youngsters would beg "Let's go for a trolley ride!" in the same way that several decades later they'd say, "Let's go to the movies." And when there was a specific destination—the circus, zoo, fair grounds, or lake—just the going there by trolley was part of the fun, a time of heightened anticipation and excitement. Baseball and trolleys have always been particularly intertwined: to ride out to the ball park on an open trolley was to feel a tingle of exhilaration, and riding home—sunburned, hoarse, and enjoyably tired—was just the right finish to the afternoon. For many a youngster, in the days before automobiles grew common, a streetcar ride was the prelude to almost every kind of outing. A few blocks away from the end of the car tracks there'd be *real* country, fine for picnics, hikes, and the imaginative stalking of game suggested by Ernest Thompson Seton's *Life in the Woods*.

On most small trolley lines, moreover, there was an endearing tradition of informality, very different from the bleak impersonality of big steam railroads. When a regular rider didn't make it to the stop on time in the morning, the motorman would dally while he came puffing up. Mr. Perkins, the daytime conductor, could be bribed by the gift of some oven-fresh popovers into leaving a parcel at Mrs. Zimmerman's house, a dozen blocks away, or into dropping a letter in the slot at the depot. Most of the time the trolley's regularity was exact enough to time the events of domestic life; by the screech of the wheels on the curve down the street at quarter to six you knew that Pop was coming home from work. If you were lying awake in the darkness, the sound of an owl

car rumbling by gave a measurement to insomnia. And when a mother couldn't leave a sick baby, a motorman would gladly convey the ipecac prescription to the druggist's.

This agreeable informality was only partly exaggerated in Fontaine Fox's "Toonerville Trolley," a beloved cartoon series that began in 1908 and speedily became a national favorite. Some of its success was certainly due to the inspired invention of the irascible Skipper, Mickey Himself McGuire, the terrible tempered Mr. Bang, and Aunt Eppie Hogg, the fattest woman in two counties. But another and important element was the manner in which the Toonerville trolley itself, wildly decrepit even in the early days, accurately reflected the public's feeling toward its trolleys—a feeling so warm and friendly that cheery derision was its natural manifestation. (In a parallel case the British, who have long had a furtive affair with steam trains, have taken enthusiastically to Rowland Emmett's drawings that show trains of monumental decrepitude.)

The extent of this friendly feeling toward the trolley is not always fully remembered today. Testimony taken from a confirmed anti-trolleyite (the son of a teamster, perhaps) might put it all down to retrospective sentimentality. "Nuts to a warm, friendly feeling," he says disagreeably. "All this selectively omits the other side—the endless waiting on windy corners, the savage crowding and stale smells, the piercing

THE TOONERVILLE TROLLEY THAT MEETS ALL THE TRAINS-3-31

WOT IF IT DOES SAY 'SHAKE WELL BEFORE USING'! DIDN'T THE SKIPPER BRING IT OVER ON THE TROLLEY!

McNaught Syndicate, Inc.

F. Fox

New Orleans until 1951 really had a streetcar tagged Desire.

THE TOONERVILLE TROLLEY THAT MEETS ALL THE TRAINS—11-27

WOODEN DO NO GOOD T' TRY TO STOP HER HERE....

'COS THE BRAKES AIN'T WORKIN' BUT SHE'LL STOP HERSELF AT THE TOP OF THAT HUMMOCK.....

AND ROLL RIGHT ON BACK DOWN TO US!

McNaught Syndicate, Inc.

squeal of the flanges on a curve, the ugly snarl of wires overhead, track all over the street, the bone-shaking ride on hard seats, the rattling windows, and above all the *slowness*."

Like so many disagreeable people, he has a point, and yet in total he is wrong. Long before trolleys came upon evil days they had acquired thousands of admirers. From the turn of the century, open cars were particular favorites with the public, prized for summer-evening jaunts. Riding an open car was cool and exciting, and the night air blew against your face with a special magic. A ride on an interurban could also be a cherished experience—winding through the woods and farmland in a powerful electric car, with its deep-toned air whistle ordering lesser vehicles off the crossings far down the right-of-way. There was a time, before the nation grew infatuated with its automobiles, when trolleys were our love.

For some, it wasn't so long ago. Just a few years back an old woman was knocked down by an auto on a Chicago street. Hospital authorities found her reticent at first about her address. She carried a bankbook that showed deposits of more than 8,000 dollars, and she admitted to being seventy-nine years old, without living relatives. She made a living selling hair nets on the streets and in taverns. But where was her home? The hospital officials finally coaxed out the answer: she spent her nights sleeping on the

It became more worrisome for interurban motormen to cross busy roads. Hagerstown & Frederick line in Maryland.

streetcars and had done so for more than seven years. "There's no law against it," said the old lady defensively, "and besides I always pay my full fare." She'd tried a number of lines, but her favorite was one that ran from Catalpa Avenue on the north to 19th Street and Morgan Avenue on the south. A good night's rest took six 17-cent tokens, paid the conduc-

tor in advance so her sleep needn't be interrupted. It was cheaper than paying fifteen or twenty dollars a week to some firetrap rooming house for a lonely, ugly little room. She'd tried rooming houses years before, the old lady concluded, but they just couldn't compare with the warm, companionable pleasantness of the Catalpa Avenue car.

The "Berkshire Hills" revealed picture-window expanses of glass. The mannerly gents in white hats were the crew.

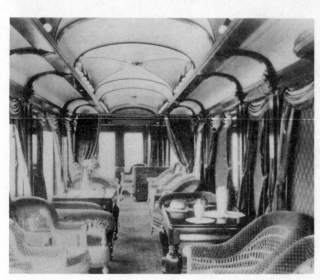

Deep carpeting and sumptuous appointments inside the Berkshire Street Railway's highly prized parlor car.

Dallying in Housatonic Village about 1905, "Berkshire Hills" showed the tasteful elegance of its curved-glass end doors.

From magnificence to meatballs, or how the mighty hath fallen. It can be argued whether simple survival is worth its price.

2. THE ANIMAL RAILWAY

The well horses we work the same hours each day, on routes that are suited to them. Fitty and low-bred horses, and those that cannot stand the sun, are assigned to early and late trips.

—Horsecar superintendent

IT IS the custom now to think of a horsecar as mildly ludicrous—a piece of engaging naïveté like a bustle or a sperm-oil lamp. But in 1886 there was nothing remotely ridiculous about horsecars. There were 525 horse railways in 300 cities and towns of the United States then, powered by 100,000 animals. They had begun to affect the patterns of city growth, for they allowed a workman to commute 6 or 8 miles, instead of being tied to a tenement close to his job. After fifty years of design development, the cars themselves had evolved into highly practical vehicles, adapted to people and horses alike.

Cars had also begun to specialize. Plush extra-fare parlor cars for refined passengers appeared. There were genteel cars for ladies only, safe from the annoyances of coarse language and tobacco smoke. Double-decker cars were tried out on high-traffic runs. Special horsecars carried mail, mixed freight, sheep, chickens, and sand or gravel. Horsecars could be rented for weddings and outings, as could black-cur-

Battle Creek's first streetcar was a proud thing for high-collared driver Johnny Ayres. The power plant was named Maud.

A horsecar hearse, made in the U.S. for use in Buenos Aires.

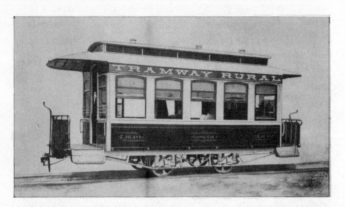

This horse-drawn sleeping car ran on a 90-mile Argentine line.

Cozy straw on the floor comforted Bostonians aboard this elegant horsecar. Advertisements inside were a brand-new idea.

Puck, the weekly, found fine material in New York's omnibuses.

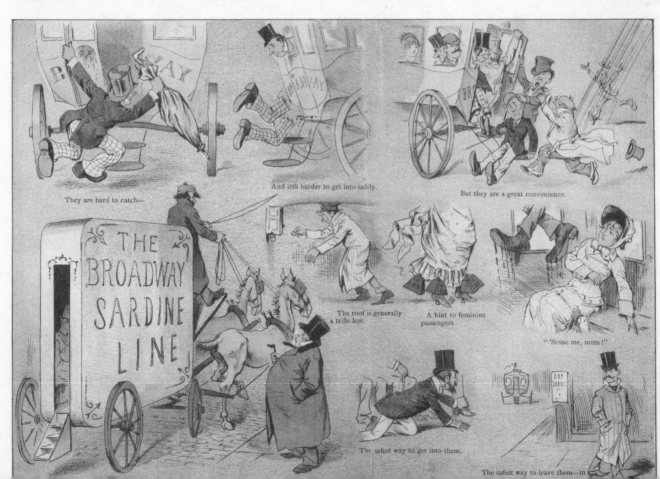

They are hard to catch—

And still harder to get into safely.

But they are a great convenience.

The roof is generally a trifle low.

A hint to feminine passengers

"'Scuse me, mum!"

THE BROADWAY SARDINE LINE

The safest way to get into them,

The safest way to leave them—in

Horsecars clopped along shaded roads in Martha's Vineyard.

tained horsecar hearses, supplied with drivers of guaranteed decorum. Once a sleeper horsecar was built in Philadelphia, for export to Argentina, which could gently bear eight slumbering passengers to their destinations.

Having a horsecar line to ride was a distinct convenience in the seventies and eighties—one of the advantages of urban life. When you stepped into the street to signal the driver, he didn't ordinarily come to a dead stop, this being a consideration usually reserved for the aged, infirm, or female. Other persons just swung easily aboard as the team slowed down a moment before resuming its 6-miles-an-hour pace. The burly driver directed his horses with fierce cries of *Gorrup!* or *Hoe!* and used both his gong and lungs to clear the track ahead, hollering an angry "Look out for the car!" at anything that threatened to intersect his course. With luck you found a seat inside on one of the two long benches, paid the conductor your nickel, and settled back to enjoy this fine, modern facility of a railway that ran right down the street. For all that the track was light and the springing primitive, it was a comfortable, pleasantly swaying ride. In the passenger compartment there was a special horsecar smell, blending the odors of smoky coal-oil lamps, sweating horses, and the pungency that came when the straw on the floor was dampened with many a dollop of tobacco juice. It was a vehicle, incidentally, where the special view of the times toward tobacco was neatly exemplified. To smoke within the car in the presence of women was held to be unacceptably gross behavior, and a man who had to have a cigar stayed on the back platform. But there are limits to the restraints that can be laid on a man, and a cheekful of chewing tobacco was entirely permissible.

Horsecars grew thoroughly tobacco-stained. Inside, the straw provided a limited absorbency. Up front the driver squirted his tobacco forward, some of it landing on the dash, some on the horses' rumps, and the rest atomizing in the breeze to float back over the car. Out on the back platform the conductor also had *his* cud, traditionally used as a weapon-within-the-law with which to dislodge impudent lads caught stealing rides by clinging to the rear of the dash.

The early days of the horsecar are shadowy. It was an offshoot of the horse-drawn omnibus, a city vehicle that first appeared in the 1820s. Before then, if a man wanted to ride within a city he hired a hack, or else walked. The omnibus—meaning, literally, "for all"—was a bright new idea: a collectively occupied public hack with its driver perched up on top. It followed regular routes and could be hailed by anyone with a few pennies in his pocket. Omnibuses were immediately successful, for cities had grown to a size where walking could be inconvenient.

From almost the beginning, though, people found fault with omnibuses. They were rough-riding, cramped, slow. The *New York Tribune* observed that "the arrangements for shooting passengers out into the mud are unsurpassed." The earliest fare-collecting method was for the passenger to make his way up the aisle to the front and thrust his fare at the driver via a little trapdoor in the roof. This was so awkward when the bus was crowded that small boys were hired to stand in back to take fares. These urchins were the first rudimentary conductors.

Street railways challenged the omnibus from al-

In design the earliest horsecars were heavily influenced by omnibuses and even stage coaches. The door was in the rear.

Boone, Iowa, in 1883. The horse was a bit small for his job.

most the beginning, though without much success for twenty years. One of the very first appeared in Baltimore in 1828, and another line began creaky service in Coney Island a few years later. The best-known early line started running in Manhattan in 1832 on a mile of track between Prince and 14th Streets. Ultimately it ran downtown from the northern outskirts of the city at 23d Street. It was really a southern extension of the New York and Harlem Railroad—horse-powered because the city fathers ruled that so perilous an object as a steam locomotive could not be tolerated in built-up areas. The first car, the *John Mason,* was a thirty-passenger stagecoach-on-rails, designed and made by a young New York wagon builder named John Stephenson. Pleased with the car's looks—it had paintings of great elegance on its side panels—Stephenson applied for and received a patent, signed by President Andrew Jackson.

In carrying capacity and riding comfort, horsecars had it all over omnibuses. Rails were a new expense, of course, although they were then only primitive iron strips laid on stone blocks or wooden stringers. They restricted the car to a fixed route, and brought such strange new complexities as switches, turn-outs, and turntables. Still, iron wheels on iron rails could haul far bigger loads than wheels running free on cobblestones and mud. Stephenson was so struck by the possibilities of the "animal railway" that he expanded his little firm to build the new cars—and went resoundingly broke in the depression of 1837. A man of honesty and conviction, he got permission from his creditors to resume building wagons and omnibuses, paid off his debts in six years, and, forty years later,

achieved a full measure of vindication. By then the horsecar dominated city transportation and Stephenson had become the most famous car builder in the world. He also became a grand old man of the industry, given to sonorous pronouncements about the unsuitability of electric motors for streetcars. He survived until 1893, to see his big factory cranking out twenty-five trolley cars a week.

What held back horsecars in the early years was a kind of massive opposition to change. Omnibuses were acceptable because they were just a kind of intracity stagecoach, and thus not really untried. But in the view of substantial citizens, these iron-track cars were radically new and very probably dangerous to the established order. The metal strips in the streets would likely cause carriages to turn over. It was felt that property value along such streets would be injured, trade in stores would fall off, and car-riding would cause the lower social orders to become still more contentious. Besides, what was wrong with things as they were?

These attitudes induced a flurry of injunctions and court actions when horsecar lines began to be widely considered in mid-century. In Philadelphia and Baltimore, among other places, there were sharp legal battles between pro- and antihorsecar factions. A Baltimore druggist, apparently fiercely determined to stop horsecars, planted himself in an armchair in front of a track-laying gang and refused to budge, being spelled in this enterprise by his wife. The impasse was resolved after some delay when it was discovered that the druggist's objections weren't generalized ones; he just claimed title to some of the land to be used on his corner. The company, hastily paying him 300 dollars, got on with the track-laying.

Once they were running, the new cars speedily overcame local objections. Their schedule speeds of

Stephenson's 1832 horsecar had three separate compartments.

Many an early horsecar line ran from the railroad station to the beach, like this mule-powered craft at Ortley Beach, N.J.

about 6 miles an hour were faster than those of omnibuses, and the ride was smoother as well. Property owners and merchants were mollified by the discovery that the new cars actually improved land values and trade. It was, moreover, a day when the steam railroad was the last word in glamorous modernity, and anything on rails shared some of its prestige. By the early fifties horsecar lines began to spread over Manhattan and Brooklyn. In 1856 they appeared in Boston and Cambridge; Philadelphia opened its first line in 1858; and by 1859 the cars were spanking along in Cincinnati, Chicago, and Pittsburgh. Soon they were running in small towns as well, typically going from the depot or steamboat wharf down the main street, past the chief hotel, and terminating out by the beach, Camp Meeting Ground, or the cemetery. (Cemeteries have always been reliable "traffic generators" for streetcars.) Often the first line in a city offered free rides for a week or two, in order to accustom people to the new cars. This practice wasn't as shrewd as it seemed, because it was difficult to start collecting cash for a service that had been free. In 1856 the first line in Cambridge built up a daily patronage of 2,000 delighted riders during its free interval; but when fares were first demanded, the delight gave way to an incensed outrage that brought rioting and offers to lynch the impertinent streetcar men.

In design the first horsecars showed strong omnibus influences, just as omnibuses had reflected stagecoaches. For example, cobblestones had called for big wheels, so omnibuses had needed inward-curving sides up to wheel height, and, for maximum space, outward-curving sides above. Though horsecars had no such need for wheel clearance, they had for years the same double curve to the sides. (The inward

curve at the sides did help cars ease past bulky drays.) "Yellow-belly," a slang term for horsecars, seems to have come from the custom of painting these vestigial wheel-clearance panels a bright yellow.

The driver rode high up on a seat at the front of the turtle-shaped roof, using a pedal to work the brake. At first fares were thrust up to him via a little door or window, and there was sometimes a mirror to help him see inside the car. If a passenger didn't present his fare soon enough, the driver would pound loudly on the roof with his whip handle, counting on the commotion and the stares of other passengers to shame the laggard. Change due back to the passenger was handed down in small envelopes. Drivers carried a supply of these envelopes in a box, each one filled beforehand with a marked amount of change. Disputes about change were frequent, though the driver had great psychological advantages—not many people could argue effectively when standing up in a lurching car and shouting up through a tiny door overhead. On crowded cars the fare-collecting method proved so awkward that conductors took over on most main lines.

At the end of the track a single-ended horsecar had to be turned around on a turntable or special track. To avoid this complication, ingenious cars were built with bodies that could be swiveled around without disturbing the wheels. The driver would simply pull a pin, lead the horses in a sidestep around the wheels, and reinsert the pin when the body was headed in the opposite direction. Instead of a pin, some cars were locked by a lever near the driver, to save him

The back platform was as a rule for men only. Concordia, Kans.

When a bobtail mounted the contraption in the foreground, the sturdy type at left swung it around. About 1870 in Cleveland.

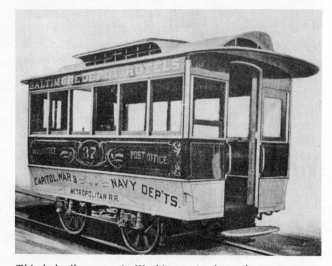

This bobtail car ran in Washington in the early seventies. A single step in the back took the place of the rear platform.

In San Francisco, Henry Casebolt's balloon cars were the kind that could swivel around without using a turntable.

the bother of dismounting. Drivers with a taste for the dramatic liked to turn around almost on the run: they'd start to swivel the car body around before it had quite come to a stop, and after a fast waltz by the horses the outfit would be trotting back the way it came, the whole performance punctuated by sharp whip crackings.

About the time of the Civil War, the omnibus-on-rails cars gave way to newer designs. The driver was moved from his high perch to a front platform, and the brake pedal changed to a brass stem-winder—a big, goose-necked crank by the driver's right hand that wound up the brake chain. Double-ended cars appeared that could be "turned around" simply by unhitching the team, walking it to the other end, and rehitching. Back platforms grew large enough to hold the riders who wanted to smoke in transit. The old turtle roof with its little eyebrow of a window forward began to flatten out and sprout tiny new windows along its sides. In 1873 the "monitor" roof appeared—a split-level structure borrowed from steam-railroad design that was stronger and gave better lighting and ventilation. Car builders became more weight-conscious. A horsecar's average empty weight had crept up to 5,900 pounds, but by the seventies it was pared down again to little more than 2 tons. The cars were sturdy enough to take outrageous overloads. John Brill, a famous car builder, wrote that twenty-two-seat cars were sometimes packed with eighty-five or ninety people.

In New Orleans in 1865 the first "bobtail" cars appeared—so named because the entire rear platform was lopped off. They were small cars designed for one-man operation and for draft by a single horse or mule. Bobtail cars were soon adopted by lines all over the country, despite general public dislike. Objectors complained that they derailed too easily, rode poorly, and were a cruel load for a single animal to set in motion. Besides, they were a regression to older days: a rider in the first ones paid his fare by walking up forward and dropping his money in a box by the driver's elbow, a procedure that in a cramped car often involved stepping on toes and exchanging brisk salvos of incivility.

But the bobtails offered so many advantages, particularly on branch lines, that horsecar companies defended them stoutly. Since they reduced labor and animal costs, service could be given where regular cars wouldn't pay. The economies also meant that cars could be dispatched more often, so there was less waiting for a car. The fare-paying annoyance was reduced by special, tilted coin chutes along the inside of the car by which a passenger could roll his coin up

By 1890 everything about a horsecar was experience-tested. Two-man double-enders like this were used on main lines.

Walking the team around a double-ender. A single iron pin (in the driver's right hand above) hitched the team to its car.

Smiling in the sun, a fine pair of mules poses amiably before one of the first horsecars to operate in Lincoln, Nebr.

to the fare box behind the driver. (These chutes fascinated those seeing them for the first time. New York horsecar men told in 1886 of a Texan so enamored of the device that he changed two dollars into nickels just for the pleasure of seeing the coins roll forward. His car had a chute at each side, and he soon hit on the happy notion of dropping a coin simultaneously into each chute and betting with passengers on which one would get to the box first. He won his stake back.) As for the criticism that bobtails were brutal loads for horses, this was flatly denied. So great an authority as John Stephenson contended that a bobtail was often easier for one horse than a regular car was for two. He observed that in most teams one horse would be a conscientious creature that would do most of the work anyhow, and the other would be a sly beast that might *seem* to pull against the harness, but only for show.

Much lore attended the purchase of streetcar horses. New York's Third Avenue Line, which kept about 1,700 horses in its stables, had a preference for gray ones, on the theory that they were apt to mind hot weather the least. Other companies had dif-

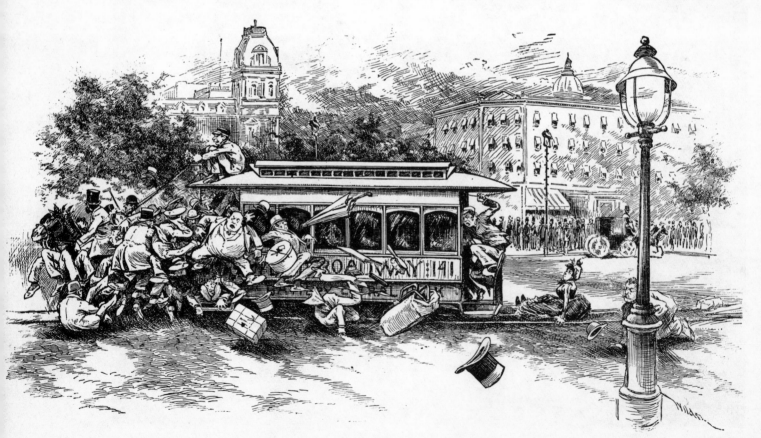

The New York rush hour in 1889, as viewed by one cartoonist. Many lines believed in the "always room for one more" theory.

ferent and conflicting color prejudices. An expert horse-buyer advised in the *Street Railway Journal* that a "man should insist on good disposition and easy gait. He should study the feet and legs, as all-important, and he should *never* buy a flat-footed horse. Color should have nothing whatever to do in the selection except to cheapen the price, as in the case of white, buckskin, or baldfaced horses." Going prices ranged from 125 to 200 dollars, and some companies had a standing offer of 150 dollars for any acceptable animal. Mules were preferred on some lines, especially in the South. They ate less, cost less, minded the heat less, and were only a little less strong. Their chief disadvantage was poor trade-in value; a horse might be resold for almost half his cost, whereas there were few buyers for elderly mules.

A line needed far more horses than cars, since horses were worked for only a few hours a day, and then as often as not in teams. In Troy, New York, the street railway kept 425 horses to pull 46 cars; in Boston the Metropolitan Railroad ran its 700 cars

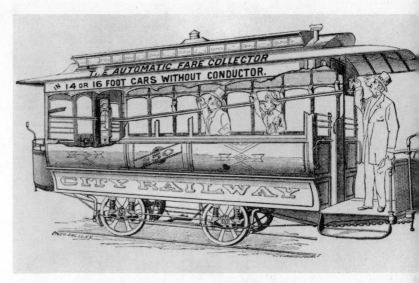

A system of patent chutes conveyed coins up to the fare box.

with an army of 3,600 horses. While cars cost more individually—a new 16-footer might come to 750 dollars—the biggest investment was usually in animals. With so much money tied up in its stables, street railways pondered long on the details of efficient management. The most crucial decision was when to sell off horses in service. (The tannery or glue factory was only a last resort, and meant that someone had miscalculated; most ex-streetcar horses returned to farm life for their last few years.) It obviously wasn't wise to keep a horse until he grew incapable, and maybe foundered gruesomely out on the line. On the other hand, elderly but car-wise horses were very good on light service, and it didn't seem right to sell animals that might work well for years. A few companies resolved this perplexing question by automatically selling horses after three or four years' service. They cited elaborate calculations to indicate that the greater cash recovery outbalanced any wasted utility. Other lines left the decision up to the practiced judgment of stable superintendents. In almost every stable there were a few animals that, by reason of special ability or charm, were exempt from the rules. Such a one was Old Crooked Tail, a remarkable beast *twenty-seven years old* described by a Chicago lady in the *Street Railway Journal* in 1885:

On March 15, 1863, a farmer of Cook County brought to Chicago a five-year-old gelding and sold him to the North Chicago City Railway. The animal was at once put to work drawing the company's cars, and continued in regular service until a recent date. He is now an "extra" and makes one regular trip of 6⅘ miles daily, with other trips as required. He has never lost a day from any cause in this long-continued service!

Our horses work seven days in the week, and this

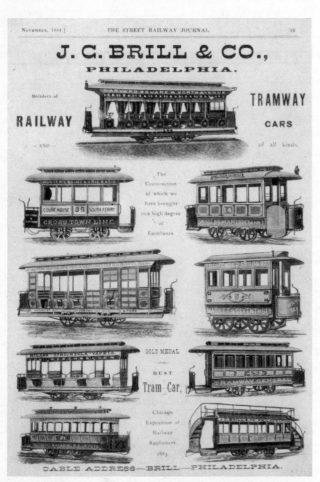

Horsecars were built in a large variety of shapes and sizes.

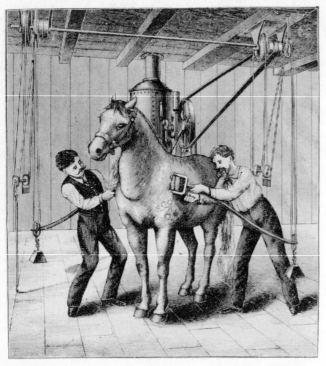

A steam engine supplied power for this grooming machine.

horse has, during the 8,545 days since he entered our service, travelled 17,090 round trips, or 102,540 miles, as a minimum, during the twenty-one years five months past. Age has not dimmed his eye! His head is as erect and he is as full of fire as many a colt!

Horsecar horses led highly regulated lives. They were stabled for nineteen or twenty hours a day, in stalls specified by industry standards as not less than 4 feet wide and 9 feet long. They munched down about 30 pounds of grain and hay a day, generally in three feedings. If a horse seemed moody or peckish, carrots, oats, and other delicacies were added to his diet. A hostler was provided for every fourteen to twenty horses, together with a shoeing expert and veterinarian for each establishment. There was also a chronic manure problem. The difficulty was less in disposing of it—manure could be sold for tidy sums, adding as much as 15,000 dollars a year to a large company's gross—than in storing it until it could be carted off. Veterinarians counseled against simply shoveling it into basement bins for storage. Piling it up outside in considerable volume brought strong neighborhood protests. The problem was never

CLARK'S PATENT POWER GROOMING MACHINE,
SINGLE OR DOUBLE.

Curry combs gave way to power tools when hundreds of horses had to be groomed. The shaggy dog in foreground is entranced.

Bursting with kids, this New Jersey car headed for the beach.

wholly solved, despite efforts to cart it off before the pile reached epic proportions. A few companies tried, without discernible success, to persuade the embattled neighbors that an enormous manure pile was not a hazard to public health, but a benefit to it, of fine germicidal properties.

Horses were expected to work 12 to 15 miles a day. By far the hardest part of the work was starting a heavily loaded car in motion; once it was rolling much less effort was needed. Hills were a second major difficulty. Long, steep grades were avoided as much as possible in laying out routes. Where they couldn't be, an extra horse was sometimes stationed at the bottom. He would be hitched on to help the team to the top, after which a "hill boy" would lead him back down for the next car. Stopping on a steep hill was tricky for a driver as well as tough on the team. It took expert timing to urge the team forward and then release the brake just as the horses lunged against the load. If the brake came off too soon, there was risk of dragging the team backward; if too late, brake drag was heartlessly added to the loads imposed by inertia and gravity.

Over the years countless inventors wrestled with both of these horsecar difficulties. Hundreds of low-friction wheel bearings were patented. One, the "Higley box," had a vogue in the late seventies and then lost favor—it was a roller bearing that worked wonderfully when new but degenerated with wear into a bearing that was worse than ordinary ones. Other inventors devised methods of converting the horizontal pull of the team into turning force on axles, using rack-and-pinion rigs, differential drums, and complexities of levers. Still other men worked hard on ways to store the energy spent on stopping a car for use in starting it up again: intricate boosters that used compressed air or vacuum, or king-size clock springs. Much of this gadgetry was unreliable

or was too heavy and costly. Though more than 2,500 patent applications for car starters had been filed by 1886, none came into general use.

A simple gadget called a "sprag" was occasionally tried on hilly lines. It was a sturdy prop, hinged at one end to the car frame and with a free end that bounced along the ground behind the car. When the car stopped on an upgrade, the brakes were released and the free end of the sprag dug in to hold the car from rolling backward. It didn't help to start up again, of course, but it did spare the team the addition of brake drag on the start.

Where a line was all mildly uphill in one direction, there was no need for animals to work on the trip back. A few lines arranged matters so that the horses or mules could ride back too. On the Cherrelyn line, in a suburb of Denver, the driver would unhitch his mule at the uphill end of the track, lead him aboard the back platform, and then coast decorously down the hill. A line in Ontario, California, did it slightly differently: its mules jumped aboard a small two-wheeled trailer hitched behind the car. The story is told of a farmer who bought some mules retired from this line and who later came storming into town to demand his money back. The mules would pull his cultivator willingly enough, he raged, but at the top of any slope they always tried to jump aboard it for the trip down.

In the seventies and eighties a well-run animal railway was capable of earning a comfortable 8 or 9 per cent. Horsecars were never as lucrative, however, as the trolley was to be. Operating costs were high,

Curtains on a Key West mule car warded off the tropical sun.

rarely less than twenty-four or twenty-five cents a car mile. This was in part because the cars were both small and slow, which meant that large numbers of them were needed, in proportion to the traffic carried. Except in large cities, most companies remained small, one-route operations, often competing with other lines that gave parallel service a few blocks away. The capital tied up in livestock was vulnerable, because a bitter winter, prolonged hot spell, or sudden contagion could disable so many horses as to put a company deeply in the red.

In 1872 the industry faced its worst crisis when a severe disease raced through the big horsecar stables in the eastern part of the country. It was called the "Great Epizootic" and it brought death to thousands of horses. For all its alarming sound, the word *epizootic* is not necessarily descriptive of a disease, and can mean simply an epidemic among animals. This disease seems to have been a particularly virulent strain of equine influenza, perhaps combined with a lymphatic infection. It first turned up in Canada in mid-October, and within a few weeks had spread down through New England, New York, and the Middle Atlantic states. By the end of November it reached Louisiana and began spreading westward. The disease baffled veterinarians, for it traveled farther and faster than could be explained by any theory of contact between horses.

At the height of the Great Epizootic, horsecar operations had to be halted in many cities. Over 18,000 horses were too sick to work in New York City alone. At one point, horses were dying in Philadelphia at the rate of 175 to 200 a day, and more than 2,250 horses died there in three weeks. The Great Boston Fire, a conflagration that burned over 67 downtown acres for a 75 million dollar loss, spread out of control in part because the disease had disabled so many fire horses. In New York City gangs of unemployed were rounded up to pull a few horsecars, and in New Bedford and elsewhere oxen—almost immune to the strange disease—were tried out. (They proved to be far too slow, and too tenderfooted for pavement.) After a few dismal months the Great Epizootic seemed to lose its virulence and replacement horses brought in from the country managed to survive. But horsecar executives long remembered 1872. Most barns stopped stabling horses head-by-head, and more care was devoted to hygienic stable management. Many officials began to think seriously for the first time about mechanical streetcars.

Cruelty to horses—apart from what was inherent in the conditions of service—does not seem to have been common. Abuse of a team by a driver was generally held to be grounds for severe reprimand or discharge. It was a day when the horse had countless public defenders, and company policies were established with an eye on public opinion as well as on the

Their work completed for the trip, the two mules of this California car boarded the caboose for their ride back downhill.

The Cherrylyn horse peeps out from his private rear platform.

considerable cash value of the beasts. Men with a native skill at handling animals were preferred as drivers, although an experienced pair of streetcar horses actually needed very little guidance. A "savvy" team of horses knew the route, responded to the tinkle of the conductor's bell, and worked in easy unison on starts and braking stops. On small lines, where the same driver and team worked regularly together, an affectionate relationship was not uncommon. Once this mutual esteem caused a derailment and considerable commotion in Canandaigua, New York. The driver involved had become very friendly with a pair of mules, made pets out of them, and taught them to chew tobacco, a practice of which they became very fond. Running out of tobacco one day, he left the car briefly, bidding his passengers and the mules to wait a jiffy while he bought three plugs.

Men proved to be costly and difficult draft animals, in this New York City experiment at the time of the Great Epizootic.

Fresh from the Pullman factory, the Saginaw horsecar "Little Jake" is rolled out to the transfer table in the plant yard.

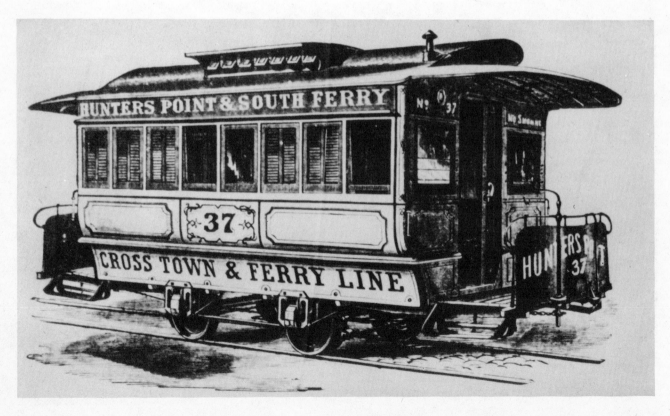

The ventilator-windows in the rounded roof spread by degrees until a two-level monitor roof became a logical development.

He was in a tobacconist's around the corner when a crashing noise outside, accompanied by screams, informed him that his friends had wrenched the car off the rails and dragged it partly over the sidewalk in their eagerness for a friendly chaw.

The easy derailment of bobtail cars wasn't always a nuisance. On cold winter nights with only a few chilled passengers riding, horsecars were occasionally known to derail near warm taverns. The cars could be pulled entirely clear of the track, freeing the rails for the passage of more dutiful cars. When the driver and his riders emerged warm and refreshed, it was no trick at all for six or eight men to pop a bobtail back on the track.

Horsecar drivers were a special breed of men, weathered and gruff. After years of teamstering animals, they normally conversed in the vibrant tones that are sometimes reserved for communicating with the stone-deaf or foreign-born. What with a brass gong to stamp on, a whip to crack, and a vocabulary of emphatic instructions in horse language, drivers generally created quite a stir. Bitter weather was the worst time for drivers, of course, for there was no heat on the platform and no protection above a waist-high dasher. On blizzardy days they wore shaggy bearskin or dogskin coats, earlapped fur hats, and an impressive array of icicles on their walrusy, tobacco-stained mustaches.

The wages for driving a horsecar were low—one dollar to one dollar and a quarter a day, for a twelve-to sixteen-hour day. The hours, at least, weren't always as brutal as they sound. There was on many lines a tradition that if riding was light, a driver could go inside the car, lie down on one of the benches, and take a twenty-minute snooze until the following car caught up with him, after which he would have to trot on briskly. Still, the duties were generally demanding. In Minneapolis, for instance, drivers were paid thirty-five dollars a month, worked sixteen hours a day for a six-day week, were required to wash the car daily, and were permitted twenty minutes for meals.

Winter heating of horsecars was a fruitful source of controversy. At first the cars simply had 8 or 10 inches of hay spread on the floor, which added scant comfort but did produce at the end of the day a minor harvest of coins and lost objects. The arrangement was also unpopular with the elegantly dressed, who usually emerged after a ride with wisps of hay clinging to their shoes. Next came small coal stoves tended by conductors, which usually overheated the

Open cars like this one built without end partitions often grew to be limber after use. The roof added little rigidity.

One explanation of why everyone faced-rearward in this 1900 Honolulu mule car was that the seats couldn't be flopped over.

A few horse lines lasted well into the electric era. This New York City car and its droopy team were photographed in 1912.

car and sometimes set everything merrily ablaze. Then the inventors appeared with a profusion of patent heaters, usually designed to fit beneath the floor or under the seats. There were receptacles for hot cannonballs, to be reheated at carbarns; kerosene furnaces that, on malfunctioning, could create dense clouds of oily soot; and chambers of unslaked lime that produced an uneasy chemical warmth but were "warranted incapable of exploding." Newspapers of the era are studded with communications from persons who felt that they had been dangerously chilled, stifled, suffocated, or poisoned on the public cars.

The to-do over heaters was as nothing, however, to the agitated controversies over snowplowing the public streets. Before horsecars, little effort had been made to remove snow from the streets. It was just packed down by traffic and ignored, awaiting a warm spell that would supply automatic removal. This was no longer satisfactory, because packed snow derailed the cars. When scrapers were first used and rock salt sprinkled along the track to encourage melting, sharp controversies broke out. Bare rails made such difficulties for sleighs and pungs that some cities flatly prohibited snow removal, at least as long as the

sleighing was good. Until enough political pressure could be mobilized to change these ordinances, many lines kept sleighs in the carbarns with which to maintain limited service. The use of rock salt stirred up hypochondriacs among the public. They felt to a man that this was a dangerous practice, injurious to the public health. It was contended that the salt made the weather along the street colder and rawer than it would otherwise have been and turned the street into a kind of gigantic ice-cream freezer. Most streetcar men said nothing, tried to keep the cars running, and prayed for spring.

Horsecars pioneered many things that would later be familiar on trolleys, including zoned fare systems, marked stopping places, straps for the seatless to hang on to, and signaling bells for passengers. On most bobtails the driver had a lever- or rope-operated system for remote control of the rear door. In the earliest days route designations were simply painted on the car body, but this gave way to destination signs on the roof, mounted on boards that could be flipped over at the end of the line. For illiterate riders or those without English, color was sometimes used as a clue to particular routes. Advertising cards in-

Out of the paint shop, with not even a scuff mark on the platform. It gave stylish service to New York's Penn Depot.

side were tried out and soon proved to be a delightful source of unearned revenue, like manure. A Boston horsecar official wrote in 1885:

Regarding signs in cars, we were often formerly applied to by ladies' church fairs, theatres, etc., and found it a great source of annoyance. Now we lease the advertising privilege and not only find it a great relief but learn that our patrons like to see the advertisements in the cars. Ladies feel gratified to have something for the gentlemen to look at, instead of staring at them. We do not ever allow dodgers to be hung up in the cars so as to strike the passengers' faces. This has brought in $4,000 per annum.

Another area of horsecar pioneering was in the effort to devise a system that would keep conductors honest. Probably one of the earliest methods of fare registering was to provide each conductor with several strips of colored paper and a punch. He was instructed to make one punch mark for each fare received, with the amount determining which paper strip was to be punched. He was further instructed to do this in the passenger's presence. Noah Brooks, a well-known newspaperman, was inspired by the posted rules of a New York horsecar line to write his famous jingle, later quoted by Mark Twain:

Conductor, when you receive a fare,
Punch in the presence of the passenjare.
A blue trip slip for an eight-cent fare,
A buff trip slip for a six-cent fare,
A pink trip slip for a five-cent fare,
Punch in the presence of the passenjare!
Punch, brother, punch with care,
Punch in the presence of the passenjare!

Abandoned on sand dunes in 1899, some of a covey of San Francisco horsecars were salvaged for use as beach cottages.

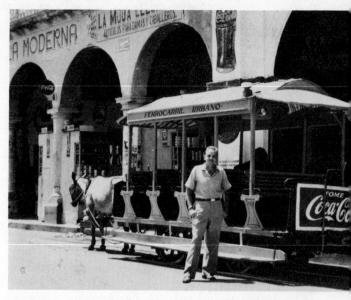

This Mexican horsecar line survived until 1952. The car here is very similar to one 80 years older shown on page 31.

Beating this system was child's play for a nickel-hungry conductor. If the passenger didn't seem to be paying attention, he could simply make a small convulsive movement with the punch, though one that left the strip of paper unsullied. Or he could employ the fine art of "double-punching," dropping one punch hole neatly on top of a previous one. So many conductors developed a skill at double-punching that by the late seventies the system gave way to more elaborate registering methods. Companies tried out bell punches, hand registers, wall registers, and other mechanisms calculated to chivvy conductors in the direction of honesty.

By 1888, horsecar lines in the United States had achieved their fullest growth, and from then on the little cars started down a steepening decline. They coexisted on amiable terms with cable cars, but not with the blue-sparking new electrics. In less than a decade the animal railway had largely disappeared, save for a few lines in protected circumstances. There was a strangely prophetic quality to their history, almost a preview of what would happen to the trolley. Beginning as a stepchild to another form of city transportation, they came on with a rush once they found acceptance. They showed a powerful capacity to change the habits of people and the shape of cities. In straitened circumstances, they countered with light, one-man cars, easily jounced from the rails. And they were finally driven to extinction by a glittering new technology.

3. WEIRD AND WONDERFUL HORSELESS CARS

No horses to buy and feed, no cable to renew, no stables to rent or stablemen to pay. No steam to frighten horses, no disagreeable dust, no fire and no smoke. No electric shocks to frighten ladies and endanger life.

—Prospectus for an 1885 compressed-air car

The steam-driven streetcar, complete with engineer, fireman-conductor, and melodious chime whistle, was undoubtedly the most dignified and conservative of all the off-beat rail vehicles to appear on American streets. Others were more peculiar. Cars propelled by compressed air, hot water, ammonia gas, naphtha, mechanical legs, and giant clock springs were all given a hopeful trial. And while some of these notions may have seemed unlikely at the time, they were scarcely more improbable to contemporary thought than proposals to run cars by electricity or by Otto engines, or to drag them along with buried ropes. Running a car by heavy-duty clockwork wasn't inherently crazier than using electromagnetism (a form of lightning) or an internal-combustion engine which, if you please, operated by deliberately encouraging explosions in its cast-iron innards.

There were several reasons why inventors sought valiantly to replace the horse during the seventies and eighties. In the first place, invention was in the air. The idea that some ingenious device might be profitable, perhaps even a way to great wealth, was more widespread than it had been before the Civil War. And the great growth of horsecar lines, despite the obvious fact that a horse really wasn't ideal for streetcar service, suggested strongly that valuable rewards were waiting. Though a noble beast and friend to man, the horsecar horse had to be worked to an extent that caused twinges of public conscience. Besides, he was slow, expensive, prone to disease, and firmly accustomed to eating whether idle or in service.

Since the steam engine was, by the end of the Civil War, a highly reliable power source, it was the natural first choice for replacing the horse. The di-

rectors of New York's Second Avenue horsecar line experimented with some primitive steamcars and found the results so promising that they relaid their track with heavier rail, disposed of their horses, and converted entirely to steam. The new "steam motors" seemed to be cheaper per car mile than horses, and faster as well. But the directors, tickled at the discovery of a power source that didn't eat when it wasn't working, forgot to allow for maintenance and repairs. Most distressingly, the steam engines began to wear out all at once, forcing costs back up until they had risen above horsecar levels. The line was ruefully reconverted to horses.

By 1876 steamcars chuffed along Market Street in Philadelphia, bearing admiring visitors to the Centennial Exposition. The Baldwin Locomotive Works had begun dabbling with the notion as early as 1873, and a car builder in Trenton, New Jersey, had turned out a few steam streetcars before 1870. It was soon evident that, however promising such cars seemed to be, they had serious problems. Property owners along the route complained bitterly about noise, smoke, and soot; and sometimes this discontent built up to injunctions or threatened franchise revocation. Since wheel loads were higher than with horsecars, better track was usually necessary. Passengers were uneasy about sitting close to boilers and fireboxes. And passing horses, a conservative-minded class of animals, tended to be upset by chuffing noises, moving connecting rods, and white plumes of exhaust vapor. Steamcars won a nasty reputation as runaway-causers.

The Baldwin Locomotive Works, pondering these drawbacks, brought out improved models that received a trial in many cities. Some were passenger-

Dummy No. 1, known as "Little Kate," waits with its two horsecars by the New Broom Hotel, Ogden, Utah, in 1889.

carrying vehicles with the boiler partitioned off at one end. A commoner kind was the separate steam "dummy"—a little four-wheeled locomotive that could tow several horsecars. It was so named because it had a boxy little false body intended to deceive horses into thinking it was an ordinary car. A typical dummy had a 7-foot wheelbase, a vertical boiler, and a 2-cylinder steam engine. Anthracite or coke was supposed to "abate" smoke and soot. Exhaust steam was led into special mufflers or to roof-top condensers, to avoid agitating horses. Aprons over the connecting rods on the wheels concealed them from the sensitive equine gaze.

Steam dummies won a small but solid position as streetcar power. Philadelphia, several New Jersey cities, and more than a dozen Southern communities accepted them for years. As late as 1899 more than seventy-five dummies were regularly in use in the United States. However, they never fulfilled their promise. John Brill, of the big car-manufacturing firm bearing the family name, wrote that "steam never really overcame the prejudice that people had in favor of horses. The [supposed] requirements of the horse were always the deciding element. Smooth pavements were out of the question because the horse would not have as good a footing as upon Belgian blocks. Steam motors were often condemned simply because people were convinced that they would frighten horses." Apart from the horse-centric philos-

ophy that annoyed Mr. Brill, steam dummies also never overcame their liabilities of cost, weight, and smoke.

But the dummy's difficulties were highly stimulating to inventors. Clearly the thing to do was to retain the excellent steam engine but eliminate the objectionable fire. "Fireless locomotives" were repeatedly proposed and were occasionally given a trial. They used thickly insulated boilers that were filled almost to the top with superheated water, confined under pressure. At each end of the line were big stationary plants to recharge the boilers. Although these locomotives could store enough energy to make 14-mile runs with ease, they were heavy and expensive. They also wasted money by cooling down overnight or when out of service. They never found much streetcar acceptance in this country, although steam railroads sometimes used them for switching in terminals and in factory buildings where smoke and fire would have been a nuisance or a danger.

Another frequent proposal was to fit a streetcar with tanks of compressed air to run the steam engines. Big compressors were envisioned at strategic points along the route, driven by steam engines or, if possible, by water wheels (the energy-for-nothing aspects of water power always fascinated nineteenth-century inventors). A streetcar would take on its charge of highly compressed air, it was suggested, and then go gliding off to carry its fares in speedy cleanliness. Apparently no high-pressure air cars were built in this country, though they had a trial abroad. There they proved to involve one of those design dilemmas that so often plague inventors: to get more than a short operating radius, it was necessary to use extremely high pressure, and this in turn brought such troubles as overheated compressors,

Two West-Coast dummys at the turn of the century. They were essentially small locomotives disguised as horsecars.

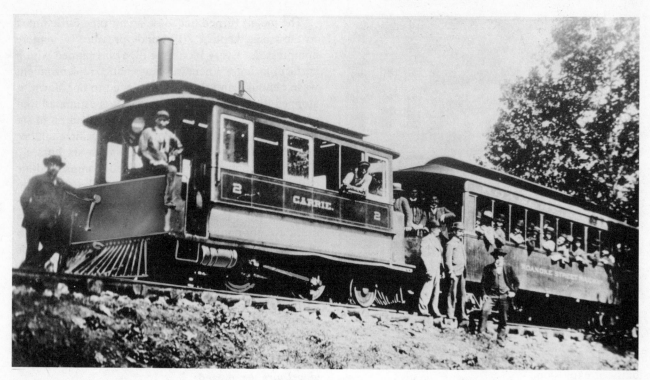

Some dummys grew uppity. This six-wheeler, with cowcatchers at each end, ran between Roanoke and Vinton, Va., about 1885.

Four wheels, each one powered, proved adequate in most cases. This fine specimen chuffed on the streets of San Francisco.

This experimental compressed-air car won a trial in Manhattan.

heavy and expensive equipment, and the distinct possibility of explosion.

In the United States a variant idea, that of streetcars driven by low-pressure compressed air, did get a trial in Cincinnati in 1885. A special car was built with a double floor, rather like a double-bottomed ship hull, that could serve as a large air tank. Tested to withstand 125 pounds per square inch, it was ordinarily pumped up to a maximum of about 80 pounds. "By a simple contrivance," its promoter reported, "the motion of the car continually replenishes the constantly exhausting air, but, of course, only partially. Means must be provided for refilling."

The means turned out to be an air pipe buried next to the track, kept at 80 pounds pressure by remote compressors. Every block the pipe was tapped with a surface fitting. Whenever automatic replenishment wasn't enough and the car threatened to bog down, it stopped to get pumped up again. "It is estimated that connection can be made and pressure taken on in six seconds, and that eighty pounds in the air chamber give the car a propelling force equal to six horses." This cheery optimism was unjustified; compressed-air cars never got out of the experimental stages. The closest they came was some years later in Rome, New York, where a fleet of little air cars operated for almost twenty-one months. It was found that two minutes of charging could give them enough power for about forty-five minutes of docile running. But their efficiency was low, and the capable trolleys took over.

The same pattern of exciting prospect and depressing result marked the ammonia-powered streetcar, product of the Standard Fireless Engine Company, of New Orleans. In the summer of 1886 the *Street Railway Journal* reported:

Ammonia gas is the active propelling agent. This gas, which is a little more than half the weight of air, is powerfully expansive, and when passed through the cylinders of a steam engine, will operate just the same as steam. . . . It is carried in a strong iron reservoir under the floor of the car. The gas is forced by powerful pumps into the reservoir until a pressure of 180 to 200 pounds is reached. Each car is supposed to carry enough gas to make one trip back and forth between Carrolton and Canal Streets.

Let it be understood that the engine is not a separate

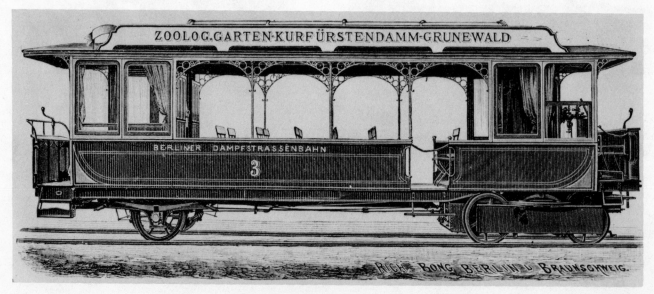

By the eighties some British-made steam streetcars achieved a scrolled and curtained elegance. Some were used in Berlin.

One version of the naphtha car. The doleful man is the driver.

matter from the car, as is the steam dummy, but each car is its own engine also. There being no fire, no smoke, no steam, no heat, there is no need to have the propelling appliances separate from the passengers. The engineer or driver sits on the front platform, which is no more encumbered than is the platform of a horsecar, and by means of a couple of levers he reverses or forwards the engine movement at will.

The *Journal* reported itself particularly impressed with some features of the design (the fact that Standard Fireless bought a number of full-page advertisements may have helped). The most applauded feature was the "provident" way in which the ammonia, after use, was not simply exhausted into the atmosphere but was instead absorbed in a water tank for re-use later.

Like the Cincinnati air car, the New Orleans ammonia car was highly impractical, even if theoretically workable. For even partial success it would have needed extremely fine workmanship in its engine and plumbing. Leaky fittings and hissing glands were ills that engineers were to be heir to for fully fifty years to come. In the pressure-generating steam boiler, frequent minor leaks were only a nuisance; with stored-pressure vehicles they were nearly fatal. (Fatal might literally have been the situation, incidentally, if high-pressure ammonia gas had blown off inside a crowded car.) As future inventors were

to discover, a streetcar is the last place in the world for a delicate mechanism. Grinding along all day over rough track in heat or cold, rain or dust or slush, a streetcar needed machinery that was at least as durable and as indifferent to abuse as a pair of good mules.

One of the most fascinating valiant-try vehicles was the Connelly Motor, a modified horsecar that spluttered and banged along Brooklyn streets for a few weeks in early 1887. It had a true internal-combustion engine fueled by naphtha, then a little-known petroleum derivative willing to explode with impressive violence. The "naphtha fluid is aerated and put into the engine in the form of vapor. The engine is a 2-cylinder machine that drives the car by means of friction gearings and a countershaft." Its advocates, unwilling to risk repelling investors by talk of explosions, mentioned only in passing that the car "operated by Otto engine principles."

Fitted to a standard 16-foot horsecar, the naphtha engine was clearly the product of much loving thought. A flywheel "capable of storing eight horsepower" helped get the car in motion, as did a special spring coupling "capable of one full revolution before transmitting power." The gearing was proportioned to give a top speed of 10 miles an hour. The horrid chance of a mechanical runaway was guarded against by an "automatic governor that causes naphtha to be admitted to the cylinders only as required, say once every eight or ten revolutions when running light."

Little is known about the naphtha car beyond the fact that it did manage to bang along the track of the Brooklyn, Flatbush & Coney Island street railway for a short time. It is possible that overheating may have

Improved naphtha car gave the driver some more platform space.

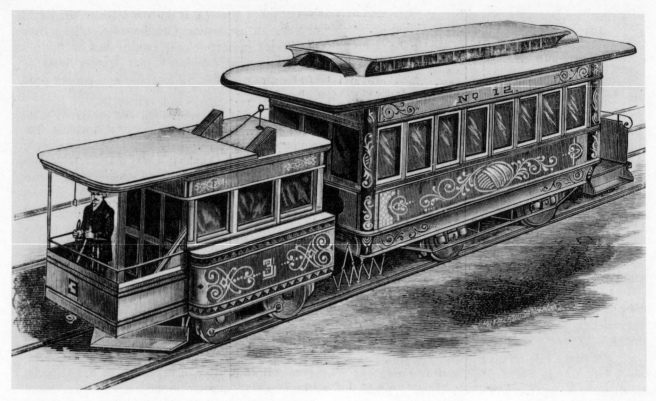

A system of patented feet beneath the Pole dummy would tramp along if the driving wheels slipped on wet or greasy tracks.

reduced it to a heap of cracked or melted metal. Or its incompatibility with nervous horses may have been a fatal flaw; even horses that regarded steam dummies with tolerance would have been scared out of their wits by a fusillade of naphtha explosions. In any event, the car was a brilliant but hopelessly premature relative of the millions of autos, buses, and trucks that, beginning a quarter century later, were to close in upon the streetcar and very nearly drive it from the streets.

A somewhat feebler grip on reality characterized other horse substitutes. One was a device called the "Pole Street Car Motor." It is not clear whether the device was named after a Mr. Pole or whether the word referred to propulsion by poling, as in a punt on the Cam. Its inventor, perhaps Mr. Pole, had a distrust of what he called "the driving-wheel system" since it was notorious that metal wheels could sometimes slip on metal rails. The method of creating power was immaterial to Mr. Pole; his "motor" was a four-wheeled dummy that could be powered, at the buyer's option, by steam, compressed air, or even electricity. "But when the well-known driving-wheel system fails to pull on slippery rail," he advertised, "then the Motor is provided with an automatic Step or Foot action. In this action the Step is like the front

legs of a horse. It may not be generally known that the front legs of a horse perform the hardest labor." Mr. Pole, if that was his name, offered to demonstrate to prospective purchasers how, even though all wheels of the dummy were locked tight, the powerful metal legs underneath could make it stride forward irresistibly.

Another mechanical-foot car had been tried out twenty years earlier on the New Orleans City Railroad. It used a stern wheel like a river boat's, though instead of paddle boards the wheel was fitted with eight iron shoes, similar in shape and size to mule hooves. This mechanism was suspended behind the rear platform of a former mule car, its imitation hooves bearing firmly against the ground. It was turned by cranks hanging down from two long walking beams perched atop the car. On the front platform was a different iron wheel that, when spun vigorously by a human mule, waggled the walking beams and turned the metal hooves. Thanks to a gear reduction, it was possible for one indefatigable man to urge the car along at a modest pace. One proclaimed virtue was that any dust the hooves kicked up was out in back, unlike the dust raised in front by real mules. Continuing difficulties were encountered in making the hoofed wheel conform to changes in ground level. But the eight-footed contraption did tramp briefly along the Rampart and Esplanade line in 1866, with an eerie resemblance to a miniature *Robert E. Lee* churning round the bend.

Philadelphia was the scene of work on the spring-driven streetcar, which, for unknown reasons, seems to have died aborning. No less than three companies were busily developing spring motors there in 1885. Of them the Automatic Spring Motor Car & Carriage Company seems to have been the farthest along. Certainly it had elaborately developed plans: each car was to be propelled by eighty powerful springs, like those in a clock but much larger. They would be encased in eight cylinders of ten springs each, and every cylinder would have individually connectible gearing. Indicators would show how much power was available in each set of springs. The power of eighty springs would be ample, the company was confident, for a trip of at least 8 miles.

There was to be no nonsense about careening off lickety-split when the springs were freshly wound. A governor would limit the top speed of the car, and besides, prudent practice would call for the use of only one set of springs at a time. "Extra sets of springs can be brought into play, however, by working a lever, in case more power is needed for grades." There was also a suggestion that downhill running and some braking stops might be used to wind up the springs a bit. But regular brakes were provided, "very powerful and capable of locking both axles, thus stopping the car within the space of six feet."

The possibility of spring breakage was admitted but belittled: "Breakage of one spring would reduce the power of an eighty-springed car only one-eightieth part. At the end of the route the broken spring would be repairable at the cost of $5, in two hours. . . . Not more than two good stationary steam engines of 15 to 20 horsepower will be necessary to any ordinary city railroad to wind the springs. The steam engines can be placed at both ends of the route, and when not in use for winding, can run the company's repair shops."

The outcome of this pleasing invention is a mystery. The last word from American Spring Motor was a report in February, 1885, by a company director named Francis Bacon: "As with every new thing, difficulties have occurred which were not expected in the beginning. At the present time nearly all perplexities have been removed; the springs have been made and tested; a large car (except for the top or wood part) completed; and a final test will be made just as soon as the machinery can be properly adjusted."

After that, silence.

It may have been that the large car, its eighty

When a man on the front platform spun his hand wheel, the big stern wheel turned. Uneven ground broke off the "feet" in back.

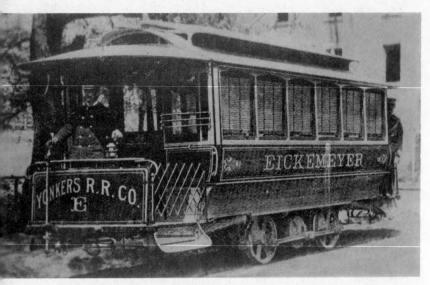

The connecting rods at the sides of the wheels performed an intricate dance when these cars waddled through Yonkers.

springs coiled tensely and its governor disordered, shot arrowlike through Philadelphia and into the Schuylkill River. It may be that it was totally destroyed in fiery collision with a puffing steam dummy. Such a climactic destruction would be far better than to have so fine a dream die prosaically of broken mainsprings.

This same minor chord, somewhere between originality and gentle lunacy, turned up occasionally even after electric motors took over. A man named Eickemeyer, for example, decided in the early days of electric cars to have no part of conventional methods of gearing motors to wheels. He devised instead an intricate system with cranks and connecting rods that thrashed about outside the wheels with considerable abandon. This gave Eickemeyer cars, which ran in Yonkers, New York, a peculiar ducklike waddle that was capable of making normal passengers queasy and queasy ones panicky. Mr. Eickemeyer also showed his originality by refusing to number his cars—he preferred to allot them letters of the alphabet—and by hiring as his assistant a penniless, young hunchback immigrant named Charles Proteus Steinmetz, whose reputation as General Electric's most distinguished mathematician was still far ahead.

Another example of uncontrollably original thinking was the "surface-contact system." This was a method of delivering electricity to streetcars that began with some fundamental design drawbacks and then exercised enormous ingenuity in trying to get around them. It consisted of a series of electrified buttons or studs, set almost flush with the surface of the street between the rails. A "skate"—a long metal

shoe—was attached beneath the car to press against the buttons as it slid along. The skate was long enough so that it would always be touching at least one button. No overhead trolley wires were needed.

The drawback, obviously, was that while it was essential for the skate to touch an electrified button, it would have been lamentable for people or horses to do it. The ingenuity came in some wonderfully devious methods of insuring that each button became electrified only when a car was above it. Switches were built into each stud that were supposed to cut the current after the car had passed. The upper face of some studs had little doors, remotely like the tiny doors in front of keyholes, and these gave endless trouble in icy weather. Other versions made use of strong electromagnets under every car to operate magnetic switches within the studs, and the magnets reaped a fine harvest of nails, scrap iron, and used horseshoes. It was found that the surface-contact system could be made to work after a fashion, but it was soon abandoned in this country. In England, where winters were milder and civic objection to overhead trolley wires stronger, surface-contact systems remained in use for years.

Some off-beat cars lasted well into this century. One of them was a strange craft that heaved into view in 1905 on the St. Joseph Valley Railway, a whimsical interurban meandering out from LaGrange, Indiana. The line, owned as a hobby by Dr. Herbert R. Bucklen, a patent-medicine millionaire, was locally known as the "Arnica Salve Line." The 1905 car was a fanciful gasoline-electric vehicle, in some respects a forerunner of the diesel-electrics that now boss the American rails. It had a primitive 9-ton gasoline engine, capable of delivering 70 horsepower at 325 r.p.m. when all went well; a 3-ton generator; and four big General Electric motors in the trucks. To

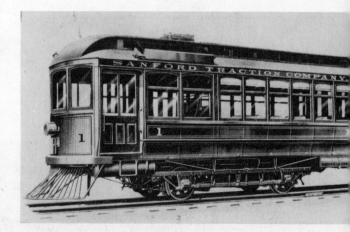

An early gasoline engine spluttered inside this self-propelled car, which ran on the "Celery Belt Line" at Sanford, Fla.

The prosperous proprietor of Indiana's "Arnica Salve Line" owned, among other oddities, this gas-driven interurban.

In Guatemala City, a Model T Ford engine urged this ex-horsecar along. Crew consisted of driver, conductor, and auditor.

help out on acceleration and grades, it also had a large storage battery. When it became evident that there was virtually no room for passengers—two-thirds of the car was engine room, and most of the remainder was filled with storage batteries—it was concluded that the car was really meant to be a locomotive instead. It seems to have given service as such for a few years.

The Arnica Salve Line, parenthetically, had a unique flavor. At one time or another Dr. Bucklen was unable to resist the urge to purchase steam engines, trolleys, gasoline-electrics, battery-electrics, and gasoline cars. The latter, having neither cranks nor starting motors, were brought to life each morning by inserting a 12-gauge shotgun shell in a chamber over one cylinder and then whacking the chamber with a hammer; the pellets, it was observed, were discharged in due course out the exhaust pipe. The line was also noted for its accidents. After it lost two passengers in a collision at Inverness, Indiana, an investigator for the Interstate Commerce Commission made a long, dazed analysis of the Arnica Salve and concluded: "Under the operating conditions disclosed, it is indeed remarkable that similar accidents are not frequent occurrences on this railway." The line expired in 1918, a few months after its owner.

Independent electric cars, powered by storage batteries, were a favorite hope of many streetcar superintendents. The belief that a miraculous battery would shortly be invented was widespread in the early days of electricity, and some men never let the notion drop. Between 1910 and 1915 there was a flurry of interest stirred up by the Edison alkaline battery and by improvements in lead-acid batteries. Several hundred battery cars were built, some of which ran in New York City as late as 1933. They tantalized company managements by promising freedom from the expense of generating and distributing current. No matter how warmly received, though, the little cars rarely went very far or fast, usually managing about 75 miles on a charge, or twice that if fed a midday booster charge as a kind of pickup. They were notably pleasing to elderly ladies for their easy ride and gentle starting habits. The gentleness arose from the fact that the little cars were usually too weak to behave any other way. Despite intensive engineering effort, battery cars never outgrew this decorous behavior.

The streetcar affinity for slightly demented mechanism was never better displayed than in the counterbalances sometimes used to help cars up extremely steep hills. The three most famous ones were on Fill-

Maiden run of a storage-battery car on the Dover, Rochester & Somersworth Railway (N.H.) was laden with derbied dignitaries.

Storage-battery cars had their greatest use in New York City. Lightweight construction helped conserve their limited energy.

In the Florida boom of the twenties, battery-powered street cars were to provide urban conveniences without ugly wires.

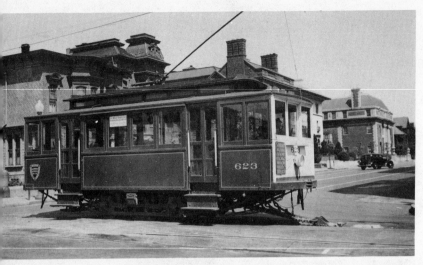

Hooked onto its subterranean cable, a trolley waits at the top of the Fillmore Street counterbalance in San Francisco.

more Street in San Francisco, on College Street, a 15-per-cent grade in Providence, and on Seattle's Queen Anne Avenue, a mean 18 per center. The principle in each of these counterbalances was similar, though there were differences in details. A sloping tunnel ran beneath and parallel to the car tracks on the steep part of the hill. Inside it, a counterweight car, nearly as heavy as a loaded trolley, ran on subterranean rails. A steel cable ran from the counterweight car through a fixed sheave at the top of the hill and doubled back down to end in a hook (at Providence) that emerged from a slot in the ground between the surface rails.

The operation had a neat simplicity. An ascending car would stop at the bottom, hook on, and then move off uphill with very little extra effort by its motors, since the car was drawn in part by the descending counterweight. At the top it would stop, disconnect, and trundle off. Along would come a descending car, hook on, and ease down the steep slope. This would both "cock" the counterbalance and reduce the extra strain on the brakes of the downhill car. The San Francisco arrangement on Fillmore Street eliminated the underground weight; in its place there was a cable rig that interconnected a climbing and a descending car, as in a funicular railway.

These unlikely contrivances worked surprisingly well. At Seattle the installation was complex, with two parallel but separate tunnels, double crossover tracks on the surface at top and bottom, and regular "hook-up men" stationed to preside over the crucial connectings and disconnectings. The device was used right up until trackless trolleys took over in 1940, and it was kept in readiness for a couple of years

longer, in case winter snows gave the rubber-tired replacements trouble. After two mild winters the sturdy old machinery was torn out and scrapped, whereupon—inevitably—snowfalls in 1943 forced temporary suspension of trolley-bus service on the steep hill.

The Providence balance ran from 1895 to 1915 and was a simpler installation. Each conductor did his own hooking on, poking beneath the car with a switch iron. Unceasing care was needed to be sure that the counterweight didn't get loose at the top of the hill, because it could thunder down and smash into the end of the tunnel with seismic violence. On occasions when this happened, the heavy hook speeding up the hill could also add to the excitement. Once it cleanly sheared off the back wheels of a dray that chanced to intersect its course.

A peculiar variation in electric-car design was hopefully tried out in Pelham Bay, New York, in 1910. August P. Belmont, New York City's rapid-transit magnate, put up funds for the construction of a 1½-mile experimental line, running from Pelham to City Island, that was unlike anything ever built before. Cars were supported and driven by central wheels running on a single rail, and were kept from tipping (as well as fed power) by two overhead rails. But shortly after opening service, a crowded car derailed on a curve, careened into several frames that supported the overhead rails, and flopped dismally on its side. Although it was going about 30 miles an hour at the time, no one was killed. The monorail's advocates pointed out in vain that the structure hadn't been built to specifications, and that the

Recurrent anxiety about the possibilities of something breaking is reflected in the 12 clamps on the car's safety cable.

motorman, knowing he had a large load of passengers, had timidly entered the curve at too *slow* a speed, thus overloading the wrong part of the structure. This ingenious defense did not impress Belmont but the line was patched up for a few years.

Of all the queer trolleys ever built, perhaps none was stranger than the armored, gun-carrying craft that emerged from a carbarn at Fitchburg, Massachusetts, in the fall of 1896. It was modeled on the *Brooklyn,* a formidable vessel in the Great White Fleet, and it brandished two 6-pounders in barbettes astride the bows, plus a fearsome 18-pounder on the main deck. There appear to have been additional guns in the rear, perhaps to discourage pursuit. Built on a self-propelled flatcar, the armored trolley was 37 feet long and 9 feet wide. She had a profusion of portholes, a bridge, and, somewhat perplexingly, an anchor.

Whether she was seriously intended as an experimental land cruiser or was built simply as a stunt is uncertain; some evidence points each way. There were sober articles about the possibilities of such a weapon in the *Literary Digest* and the *Electrical Review.* The *Digest* called the trolley an "instrument of warfare of infinite use." The *Review* pondered that "it is not beyond the range of modern mechanics to build a car that would be bullet-proof and [that would] constitute a travelling fort. . . . It could transport men and guns from one point to another with greater celerity."

Arguing against a martial interpretation of the armored trolley are other bits of evidence:

1. It was promptly christened the *McKinley,* and saw immediate action in campaigning against William Jennings Bryan.

2. Although, as James D. Hall wrote entertainingly years later, its proponents laid great stress upon "the lead-ballasted bow whose special design, augmented by the brute force of *sixty horsepower,* could shear its way through any barricade," they apparently overlooked the possibility that an enemy force might descend upon the supply line and separate the *McKinley* from her powerhouse.

3. Inspection of surviving views of the *McKinley* reveals a small lifeboat suspended in davits on the port side. It is not clear how, in doughty defense of the republic, a lifeboat could come in very handy on an armored streetcar.

A lifeboat was standard equipment, however, on the famous sea-going English trolley that ran in the nineties from Brighton to Rottingdean. One of the most cheerfully lunatic vehicles ever built, the 36-ton *Pioneer* ran on a 3-mile track that was 14 feet

End of a bright dream: a wrecking crew props up the toppled Pelham Bay monorail car. Note the single rail on the ground.

Bent awry in the accident, the wheels on top of the car were supposed to bear sideways against the two light rails above.

Ready for a regatta, the trolley cruiser "McKinley" noses its ram up to a tall worthy who appears to symbolize Uncle Sam.

beneath the waves at high tide. It was built on four tubular steel legs and had two decks, a "sumptuous yacht saloon," and lifebelts for 150 passengers. A week after the *Pioneer* (familiarly known as the Spider, the Travelling Pier, and Daddy Long Legs) made its inaugural run in 1896, it was totally wrecked in a storm. Rebuilt the following spring, Daddy Long Legs had a successful three-year life as a tourist attraction, including one red-letter day when King Edward VII, then Prince of Wales, accompanied by the Duke and Duchess of Fife, made a happy round trip on the sea-going trolley.

First voyage of the British sea-going trolley took place on November 28, 1896, at a time when the tide was well out. It creaked along at an exhilarating 6 m.p.h. At high tide the water rose to within a few feet of the capacious main deck.

4. THE DAY OF THE GRIPMAN

A cable car has no will of its own to thwart the will and efforts of its faithful driver.

—President of a Chicago cable-car system

Anyone old enough to recall the unlikely contrivance of cords and pulleys that, years ago, was used to make change in stores will have an excellent notion of how cable cars worked. This was the wondrous mechanism that whisked your money off overhead in a tiny carriage, darting to the cashier in the balcony like a homing pigeon and then trundling back with your change wrapped in a sales slip. It was, in essential respects, a miniature cable-car system.

The first glimpse of a cable car was startling, even spooky, to a man familiar only with horsecars. Although there was nothing out in front to pull it, the car glided quietly past as if it were a magic carpet. It moved at a brisk 8 or 9 miles an hour, too, faster than horsecars had gone on all but a team's last run of the day, when the shrewd beasts knew they were headed for the stable and feedbags. It made very little noise, moving without the *clop-clop* that for decades had signaled the approach of a streetcar. Stepping into the roadway when no car was near, you could see a metal-rimmed slot between the tracks, and if the street was quiet, you could hear a mysterious slapping noise come faintly from under the ground. Riding on this newest marvel was as remarkable as watching it go by. The clean new car had none of the old sweat-and-stable smell. A fellow stood in the middle and worked several long levers extending down through the floor; when he moved one of them the car instantly started up and in no time was rolling along at full speed. All you could hear was the rumble of the wheels, the click of the rail joints, and the occasional clang of the warning gong. The car seemed to go almost uneasily fast, especially around curves, which it careened through at exactly the same pace as along straight stretches.

Much of the appeal of cable cars lay in their inherent simplicity. The principles were ones that any-one could grasp. A stationary steam engine drew an endless cable beneath the street, and a mechanism under the car could seize or release the cable at the "gripman's" direction. It was a concept ideally suited to the engineering spirit of the seventies—an enthusiastic belief that cast iron and ingenuity could work almost any miracle. Moreover, cars were clearly not likely to catch fire, explode, or give off distasteful gases. Horses that insisted on being alarmed by cable cars would be neurotic indeed. As one promoter said, extolling the ease of cable-road operation: "In the cable system we get all our passengers on a rope, and then we keep pulling the rope in. It is simplicity itself."

But by far the most eloquent definition of the new system was formulated in the eighties by Charles P. Shaw, Esq., a New York lawyer. Mr. Shaw, a full-blooded orator and master of the nonstop sentence, appeared before a special commission of the state Supreme Court to assail some anti-cable injunctions that horsecar lines had obtained. He pulled out all stops. He touched on how man is subtly influenced by the vehicles he rides—how a person feels furtive when traveling in a broken-down hack, but "asserts his sense of personal worth" when riding a stylish vehicle. Taking a deep breath, Mr. Shaw delivered himself of a 227-word sentence:

This may seem a trivial matter, but if our whole city, including its rich and poor, could be lifted up to an appreciation of a system of intramural transit, at once elegant, commodious, adequate, cheap, noiseless, cleanly and in every way pleasant, and at the same time so comprehensive and adaptive as to carry for a single fare of five cents *up* town and *down* town, on *both sides* of the city, and *across* at convenient intervals, so as to connect with all our established ferries upon the two glorious rivers that cincture our metropolitan island, in commodious and elegant cars, propelled by the noiseless and perfectly subjected power of steam, exerting its energy from an unseen and distant station, under this mysterious cable railway grip which, like the human hand, plays, if I may use the expression, the symphony of locomotion —and all this without the *noisome* products of combustion and the *noise* incident to the lumbering, vibratory energy of the locomotive, and without the faeculent voidings incident to the use of animal power, the perils of which to the health of the city have been so powerfully and graphically described before you by Professor Doremus and other sanitary authorities—I say, if all this be so, what a power for weal or woe to this city is held in your hands, gentlemen of the Commission!

But the injunctions of horsecar operators could no more stop cables than, a few years later, the obstructionism of cable roads could block electric cars. Like the squalls that often accompany a change in the weather, obstructionism has generally been more noisy than effectual in retarding streetcar development.

Cable cars were largely an American institution; and in this country San Francisco was both the first city to have had them and the last to have kept them. There, in fact, cable cars have assumed the character of a peculiar and valuable local property, just as Boston cherishes an image of culture and St. Augustine cherishes alligators. Whenever efficiency-minded San Franciscan officials have suggested that buses might well replace the remaining cable cars, a caterwaul has arisen from the citizenry comparable to that which would develop if someone proposed to remodel Mount Vernon into a ranch-type Colonial.

The peculiar local treasure was sired by a manufacturer of wire rope named Andrew Smith Hallidie. If he didn't conceive the underlying notion—mines

This was San Francisco's first cable road, photographed in Sept., 1873, a month after Hallidie made his trial runs.

had previously used cables to haul ore cars—he certainly deserves credit for devising a passenger-carrying system and for licking many design problems, including that of a workable cable grip. Nor does the fact that he was a leading cable manufacturer and thus in a position to benefit lessen his achievement any. Utter disinterestedness is not a proper requirement for inventors.

The story goes that Hallidie began work on his cable car after seeing a gruesome horsecar accident one evening in San Francisco in 1869. A heavily overloaded car was struggling up a steep hill. An extra team of horses had been hitched on for the climb, but it was a difficult haul because the car was jammed with rush-hour standees. The car reached a point where the team seemingly couldn't gain another inch. One horse, pulling hard, stumbled and lost his footing. When this happened the driver was supposed to clap on his brakes to relieve the team of the backward drag; no antirollback device was fitted to the cars. But the driver was an instant late and the car began to roll backward; when he did crank the brake on hard, it broke. The tumbled and terrified horses

Cable-company men lean negligently against a Portland, Ore., car on its turntable. "Uncle Tom's Cabin" was playing there.

were dragged backward down the hill at increasing speed. The car, still on the rails, ultimately stopped at the bottom, but the horses had to be shot. Horrified by the accident, Hallidie resolved to find some other means of hauling streetcars.

Building the first line, on Clay Street, turned out to be difficult because the workmen excavating for the cable vaults kept running into unexpected water mains and sewers, each of which had to be relocated. Before the 2,800 feet of the world's first cable-car line was done, Hallidie's shaky little company discovered that Clay Street had two sets of gas and water mains, plus several sewer systems, and a long-forgotten series of old water cisterns. Hallidie had put everything he had—about 20,000 dollars—into the cable-car company, and a few friends' savings and some borrowed money brought its total capital up to a little less than 100,000 dollars. Construction costs were unexpectedly high (Hallidie had to pay machinists and carpenters a stiff $3 *a day,* hod carriers $2, and laborers $1.50) and it grew evident that the pioneering half-mile line was going to have only one chance at succeeding.

The tryout took place at five in the morning of August 1, 1873. The early hour was less to avoid possible embarrassment before onlookers than from a sense of panicky urgency—Hallidie's franchise specified that experimental operation must be begun by that date at the latest, and he knew that minor

Andrew S. Hallidie put his entire savings into the first line.

At a San Francisco ferry, the little horsecars in the background were overshadowed by the bigger and faster cable cars.

In the middle of the front seat, wearing a tall hat, Hallidie poses before riding up his highly successful Clay St. line.

troubles and hitches were inevitable. The narrow-gauge track plunged down an alarmingly steep slope, with a grade approaching 20 per cent in spots. According to cable-car folklore, Hallidie, his three partners, and a small group of city officials stood about on the top of the hill before the first trial, waiting for the early-morning fog to blow away. When it did disperse, the workman who had been assigned to running the car on the first trip took a hard look at the steep slope, and resigned on the spot.

Hallidie took his place, spun the horizontal control wheel that worked the first grip mechanism, and slid off down the slope at a decorous but thrilling eight miles an hour. Then he brought the car back up the steep grade, stopping and restarting several times in a breath-taking display of virtuosity. Later that same day an official first run was held for numerous city dignitaries, and then the only mishaps of the tryout occurred. So many helpful hands pushed the car on the turntable that a bolt in the grip mechanism was sheared off; and during the delay for repairs the rumor spread through the large crowd that the whole invention was a complete failure. When the car was finally repaired, a total of ninety people managed to push their way aboard the grip car and its trailer—the two had seats for only thirty between them—and the wildly overloaded little cars moved off uphill. At the steepest part of the climb the cars stopped dead, unable to budge. Hallidie scurried to the powerhouse, found that the cable was slipping on its driving sheave, and saved the day by throwing sawdust and lime on the slipping cable until it began to move again.

Cable cars proved an immediate success. Stimulated by the report that Hallidie's line was soon netting 3,000 dollars a month, five or six other lines began to build cable roads in San Francisco. A respected citizen named Henry Casebolt invented a bizarre variation, in which the moving cable was suspended from poles overhead, the way future trolley wires would be. A trial stretch of "Casebolt's Elevated Cable for Rapid Transit" was built in Oakland and occasionally dragged an experimental car along for the edification of prospective investors. Although Casebolt was an established inventor—he had built some highly successful "balloon" horsecars with bodies that could pivot around the wheels and soon developed a cable-grip mechanism that displaced Hallidie's—he could raise no money for the overhead cable. Underground cables, however, did not lack for investors. In the mid-seventies the California Street line was begun, mechanically improved and esthetically dazzling. The grip mechanisms were

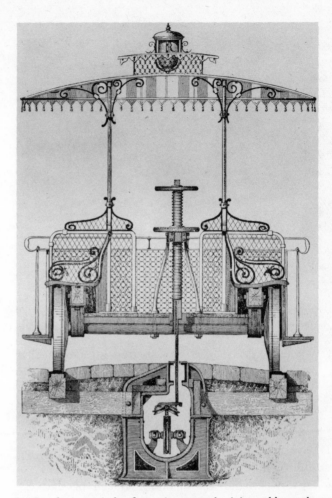

Sectional view of the first grip car and of its cable vault.

lever-operated and smoother; the cars were finished in maroon and gold, with stained-glass transoms and enough gingerbread to awe the customers, who paid five cents a ride. Completed for a staggering 450,000 dollars, it was opened on April 10, 1878. It is one line that is running still.

By the early eighties, cable cars were running in many American cities, and a visiting provincial felt a look-no-horses wonderment at the sight of them. They were faster, cleaner, and quieter than anything known on city streets before. They brought power in earnest to street transportation: great reciprocating steam engines of 500 or 750 horsepower, endlessly drawing in the heavy steel cable from its underground vaults. But like all new contrivances, the little cars had a full share of teething troubles.

The slot in the road, which had to be built strong enough to withstand the impact of heavy, metal-tired dray wheels, was one headache. It had an exasperating tendency to contract shut on cold nights or to yawn wide enough to trap narrow buggy wheels on

Cutaway view of a New York cable powerhouse. The sheaves in the foreground were designed to take up slack in the cables.

hot days. Slot "yokes"—cast-iron structures that carried the slot rails—were redesigned to compensate for temperature changes, and the slots then showed a spiteful habit of opening out on cold days and closing up on hot ones. In Philadelphia, the first cable road had such aggravated slot trouble that the first car to leave the barns on a trial run didn't get back home until months later.

Below ground, the elaborate system of sheaves, idlers, and cable guides needed regular attention. Silt and sand had to be mucked out and thousands of hidden bearings kept greased. Friction was the big enemy of the cable road. On some lines just moving the cable alone, without hauling a single car, took more than half of the total power consumed. And when something did break down, the stoppage was likely to be of epic proportions. On horsecar lines, when a team or car came to grief, the line could always be promptly cleared. With cables there were endless possibilities for mischance and the trouble usually extended far beyond just one car. When something vital broke, *all* cars stopped and the passengers debarked, after an interval of increasing impatience, with that peculiarly white-knuckled, letter-to-the-newspaper glint that city transit has always evoked.

The cable itself, the heart of the system, needed continuous care. It was immensely long; a 3- or 4-mile cable was not uncommon, and one Denver cable was almost 7 miles long. Usually 1¼ to 2 inches thick, it was typically made up of six subordinate cables of maybe nineteen steel wires each, spirally wound about a rope core and coated with tar

and linseed oil. No matter how uniformly a cable was treated, each one seemed to have a personality of its own. Some cables were docile and mannerly; others gave the splicing gangs endless trouble. Complete breakage was rare, but ill-tempered cables frazzled out with broken single wires that could snag in the machinery.

The *idea* of breakage, however, was in everyone's mind. A story went around San Francisco that a Chinese, perceiving a stalled car, once gravely asked the gripman: "Whatsa maller—stling bloke?" A new cable usually had a breaking strength of 35 or 40 tons, decreasing about 35 per cent at the end of its useful life. It was the custom to examine the cable late at night when no cars were running, inching it through the powerhouse past an inspection crew.

Cables had a way of stretching a good deal when first put into use, and then growing a little throughout the rest of their lives. This trait once made trou-

Electric motors have replaced San Francisco's steam engines, but the big iron cable sheaves are still spinning awesomely.

ble for the management of the brand-new Sutter Street line in San Francisco, which had planned a gala opening-day festival, complete with free rides for all, speeches, top hats, a brass band, and plenty of champagne in the carbarn. About 10,000 people turned out for the occasion in 1877, so many of whom piled aboard the shiny new cars that the cable promptly stretched beyond the capacity of its take-up mechanism. Every car ground to a halt, and the company had hastily to hire teams of horses to draw its guests back home. Emergency splicing crews were put to work on the cable, but it was the next day before they had amputated the 75 feet of stretch that had appeared in the cable.

A good cable was supposed to last for 75,000 miles or so, perhaps a year's use on many lines. Soon it grew evident that cable life was greatly shortened by passing it over small sheaves or pulleys that flexed it abruptly. Accordingly, whenever a street curved or the tracks turned a corner, the cable was run over a series of sheaves, spaced close together, or over two or three great 8-foot horizontal wheels beneath the road. This often meant that there were occasional "dead spots" where gripmen had to disengage and coast before they could safely retake the cable. Similar skill was also necessary where one cable intersected another.

Losing momentum in a dead spot generally meant that the passengers had to get out and push, something of a blow to any gripman's pride. The technique on approaching a dead spot was to get resolutely up to full speed, let go at the last possible instant, and coast briskly around, hoping that nothing solid would be disclosed on the tracks around the bend. The characteristic cry of San Francisco cable-car men, according to several historians, was a hoarse *"Kowfadakuv!"* Translated, this was a warning "Look out for the curve!" It was a particularly cheerful occasion

Complicated anyhow, cable construction grew tougher if horsecar service wasn't interrupted. New York City in Oct., 1891.

Heavy cast-iron yokes were buried in the ground to form the cable vault and brace the slot rail. Union Square in New York.

for the riders when some surly conductor, perfunctorily crying *"Kowfadakuv!"*, missed a handhold himself and was tossed into the street.

Sometimes longer curves were arranged so that the gripman had to hold onto the cable. To negotiate a lengthy reverse curve on New York's Broadway line around Union Square, the gripman had to choose the best opportunity available in the dense traffic and commit himself to the entire crooked stretch; he could not let go until he emerged into the straight track beyond. On this hazardous portion of the run it was the custom for a gripman to set up a wild din on his gong, augmented as necessary with profanity addressed to persons or vehicles that disregarded his noisy and relentless approach. His passengers would be lurched left, then right, then left again, and sometimes flung forward by glancing collision with a beer wagon or other slow vehicle. The section of the line became known, not entirely in fun, as "Dead Man's Curve."

Like the horsecar driver before him, the gripman grew to stature as a public personage. If the weather was fine, passengers preferred to "ride the grip"—the open grip car in front, rather than the trailer usually coupled to it. On the grip there was ample opportunity to admire the style with which the gripman manipulated his big levers, clanged the gong, and showed the same intimate knowledge of his route and its dead spots that a river pilot had of sandbars and snags. A muscular but deft hand on the lever was imperative; if the grip was engaged too timidly, the excessive slippage was bad for both grip and cable, and if it was moved too abruptly, the customers' heads would all be jerked backward in unhappy unison.

Although breakage of single strands didn't weaken a cable appreciably, it did occasionally lead to a moving car being unable to let go. A broken strand or two would tangle in the grip and the car and its trailer would go charging inexorably along, unable to stop for anything. When a gripman found himself unable to pull free by hard braking, he would jangle his gong in loud, continuous warning. Before long, he'd catch up with the car ahead, perhaps letting off or loading passengers. Its gripman, hearing the desperate alarm signal behind, would instantly start up to avoid a collision and begin clanging *his* gong too. Sometimes, according to cable folklore, as many as five or six cars would go clanging along the street, urgently fleeing the runaway at the rear of the procession. It was the responsibility of the conductor of the jammed car to leap off on the run, hunt down a new-fangled telephone, and frantically call the power-house to stop the cable. Some lines installed a telegraph system with call boxes like those of fire alarms so that a conductor could bring the stampede to a halt.

Though not uncommon, cable-car accidents were not as lethal as trolley accidents were later to be. Partly this was because traffic was light, and partly because the cars weren't much more substantial than horsecars—they didn't need weight for traction. Most important of all, they didn't go very fast. Typical speeds were 7½ to 9 miles an hour downtown, and sometimes up to 12 or 13 in residential districts. It was quite possible, though frowned upon, for an agile passenger to board or alight on the run.

These speeds, however unimpressive now, were highly stimulating in the eighties. They were a great deal better than horsecar averages and permitted a considerable lengthening-out of the radius within which a man could live and still get conveniently to work. Real-estate values, it was discovered, were actually enhanced rather than injured by a cable road in the neighborhood. Property owners often fought cable lines hard in the preliminary stages and, after losing the battle, reaped very substantial benefits.

Chicago's cable system, which started operating in 1882, soon grew to be the biggest and fanciest in the world. Building it was an enormous task by the standards of the day: the first four miles soaked up a staggering 100,000 dollars per mile, requiring 50,000 wagonloads of sand and gravel and 5,000 tons of iron and steel. On the day that service was ceremoniously opened, more than a quarter of a million spectators showed up to cheer the dignitaries and gaze at the new Eighth Wonder.

As it had been on horsecars and would be on trolleys, rush-hour crowding was a problem in every big city. The following verse had a currency in San Francisco, but it would have been understood everywhere:

Never full! Pack 'em in!
Move up, fat man, squeeze in, thin.
Trunks, valises, boxes, bundles,
Fill up gaps as on she tumbles.
Market baskets without number,
Owners easy nod in slumber.
Thirty seated, forty standing,
A dozen more on either landing . . .
Toes are trod on, hats are smashed,
Dresses soiled, hoop-skirts crashed.

Contemporary gripman in San Francisco. For eighty-odd years, his job has taken a strong, skillful touch on the big levers.

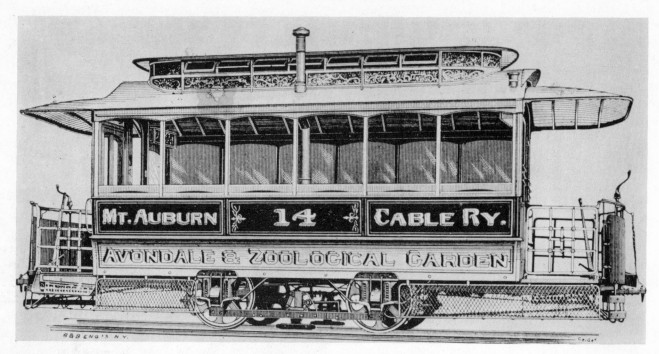

The latest thing in Cincinnati in the late eighties was this gaudy new closed cable car, with protective platform gates.

Open grip car in Cincinnati had elaborate cast-iron devices to keep the thin shank of the grip from wearing in the slot.

In its prime, Chicago had the largest cable-car system in the world. This was a half-open, half-closed "California" car.

Derailed after disputing a crossing, this San Francisco cable car is levered back onto the rails before a fascinated crowd.

the cars were not self-propelled, they showed a fine capacity for coping with bad weather, heavy snow-falls, and abnormal load peaks. Once when the G.A.R. held its annual encampment in Washington, a cable-car line heroically toted 170,000 passengers in a single day. Philadelphia, Washington, and New York all built cable networks that were nearly as elaborate as the system in Chicago. Denver had 44 miles of track and St. Louis 55 miles. There were cable cars in Providence, Oakland, Baltimore, Omaha, Seattle, Hoboken, and over the Brooklyn Bridge (three cents a ride or ten tickets for a quarter).

Although in the years of widest use cable cars operated on level streets as much as on grades, it was on steep hills that the little cars particularly shone. Not only were they first developed to climb precipitous slopes, but it is on hills that they managed to survive. Self-propelled cars can climb only where wheels will not spin on rails; but cable cars, in the form of funicular railroads, can behave like tilted elevators and ascend virtually any slope. Sometimes a form of cable car was used literally to give trolleys a lift. One famous arrangement was the Mt. Adams incline in Cincinnati, where trolleys rolled onto a movable platform, to be raised or lowered to a different level in that hilly city. The Mt. Adams

Trolleys rode their own cable cars up and down the Mt. Adams incline in Cincinnati. There was a fine view over the city.

Thieves are busy, bent on plunder,
Still we rattle on like thunder.
Packed together, unwashed bodies,
Bathed in fumes of whiskey toddies;
Tobacco, garlic, cheese, and beer
Perfume the heated atmosphere.
Old boots, pipes, leather and tan,
And if in luck, a "soap-fat man."
Aren't this jolly? What a blessing!
A street-car salad, with such a dressing.

The economics of cable roads proved curious: the lines were shockingly expensive to build but remarkably cheap to run. Operating costs were far lower than on the big horsecar lines. In Chicago it cost twelve cents a mile to run a cable car, compared to twenty-five cents a mile for a horsecar. But construction costs sometimes soared as high as 200,000 dollars a mile, as in Washington. The natural result was that cable lines were almost invariably built where traffic demands already existed and not, as with trolley lines later, where there was mainly a promise of generating future traffic.

Despite the expense, cable trackage grew steadily until the nineties. There were by then almost 500 miles of cable track in the United States, with 5,000 cars carrying 400 million passengers annually. Since

A cable car threads its way briskly across a line of trolleys and drays in Seattle. Just one horseless carriage is visible.

incline remained in use until 1947. In other places trolleys were not transported up or down but their passengers were—in Duluth, Los Angeles, and the famous old Mt. Lowe incline in California. Here for years trolley excursionists were cable-drawn up Echo Mountain from Rubio Canyon, to find refreshment in the trolley-owned Alpine Tavern at the top.

In every city where regular cable cars glided along, the hidden cable slapping along beneath the slot in the road had a magnetic lure for venturesome small boys. It was readily the subject of a dare, a heroic means for showing off. One caper was to find a board that would enter the slot and hammer into the end a pattern of nails that would engage the cable. When this end was rammed down the slot, the plank would clatter wickedly along the street like a shark's fin, scattering pedestrians, frightening women, and, with luck, encouraging horses to rear and run away. A variant was to tie together a cluster of tin cans and hook a towing wire around the cable; the cans would

Riding the cable incline to the top of California's Mt. Lowe was a popular destination on Pacific Electric trolley trips.

Specialized cable cars, shuttling up and down the famous Angel's Flight, provide vertical transportation in Los Angeles.

Before the last run of a cable car in Kansas City, Mo., in 1913. The inclined way was later replaced by a viaduct.

go bouncing and clanking off with a wonderful racket. A more malevolent stunt was to drive a wedge hard into the slot, where it might succeed in breaking the grip of the next car to come along, snarling traffic for miles around.

Daring juveniles could also hitch a ride. One method was to snare the cable with a hooked wire and, using roller skates and the stance of a water skier, catch a thrilling ride to the top of a hill. Another daring gambit was to tie clothesline to an express wagon or sled and, fishing delicately in the slot, attempt to tangle the end around the cable. When there was a good bite the express wagon would whirl excitingly along, giving the young delinquent in the driver's seat a fine opportunity to demonstrate his valor. Experienced lads kept an open knife handy, like a harpooner's axe, in case a policeman or obstacle should suddenly be encountered. Tag ends of tangled clothesline on the cable plagued cable maintainers and were found most often in the spring of the year, when the sap flows strongest in small boys.

From the mid-nineties on, cable cars were steadily replaced by trolleys. In Philadelphia and Providence

These blackened, heat-twisted trucks were all that was left of the California St. cable cars after the San Francisco fire.

the changeover came in 1895; in Baltimore, in 1897. A disastrous fire halted Washington's cable system in 1897, and horses were temporarily used to maintain service; then the decision was taken to rebuild the system as an electric one. St. Louis let its cables go slack shortly after the turn of the century. Chicago's big system managed to last for a few years longer. Wrote the Chicago *Tribune* for July 22, 1906:

Groaning and wobbling, as one decrepit and one having earned a rest, the final cable train rattled and bumped around the Loop for its last performance at 1:35 A.M. The train consisted of a battered grip car and a twenty-year-old trailer. Just behind it came the first State Street trolley car, forerunner of a faster means of transportation.

The gleaming new trolley was to flower beyond expectation and to see some remarkably dizzy years; and then it, too, would come to its time of groaning and wobbling.

Cheerfully cresting a rise in Nob Hill, a contemporary cable car in San Francisco now also serves as a tourist attraction.

Clambering aboard as the car is slowly swung around on its turntable is part of the fun. No bus can make this claim.

Though the grade here is steepened by the camera lens, first riders in San Francisco give thought to the cable's strength.

5. THE INFANT SPARKERS

. . . as yet unsatisfactory as to uniformity, control of speed, and ability to start or stop at pleasure.

—*From a report on an early electric car*

Roughly a century after Galvani discovered that frogs' legs would twitch when touched with copper and iron (a finding not in itself obviously useful), the first successful trolleys managed to grind up steep hills without invariably burning out their motors. It was a century in which scores of men dreamed of electric transportation. Toward the end of that period, by the eighties, electric cars were as repeatedly invented as space ships have been in our time, with the result that many people became a trifle impatient about the delay in perfecting them. Horse-car officials scouted the experiments for years, hopefully keeping an eye on the new art.

The basic scientific knowledge came early. After Galvani and Volta, there was Oersted who in 1820 discovered a "field" around a current-carrying wire. A decade later Joseph Henry discovered the electro-magnet; and in 1831 Faraday added the crucial finding that moving a coil through a field created electricity.

But between these discoveries and the machines to make adequate use of them stretched years of frustration. It took almost half a century to go from Faraday's announcement to a remotely practical vehicle. The miscalculation of the men who worked so hard and fruitlessly in this interval lay in the belief that electricity in powerful amounts could be obtained from a zinc-fueled battery.

The earliest of these wrong-road pioneers was Thomas Davenport, a blacksmith of Brandon, Vermont. Captivated by his first sight of an electromagnet, he bought it, studied it at length, and in 1834 built a tiny electric motor—one of the first in history. Next he built a motor that propelled itself around a little track, like a toy train. This model electric railway was exhibited in Boston and Springfield in 1835. An original and gifted person, Davenport is still recalled by faintly awed historians as the man who tore up his wife's wedding dress to get silk insulation.

Four years later another solitary original, a Scotsman named Robert Davidson, built an electric locomotive. It weighed 5 tons, carried long rows of primary cells, and had a control system of engaging simplicity. To start, Davidson unwound a crank that lowered sixty zinc plates into the cells; to stop, he cranked them up again. His locomotive once achieved a quivering 4 miles an hour on the Edinburgh-Glasgow line. Then one night at Perth it was overturned and smashed by a gang of tipsy stokers and engineers, believing in their innocence that it "threatened their employments."

In 1847 in New Hampshire a Professor Moses Farmer displayed an electric car that could carry two people. Professor Farmer, whom we will encounter again, tried a new wrinkle: instead of lugging the batteries along, he left them at one end of the track, connected to each rail. It was a natural idea, but one that was to cause endless future difficulties.

Electromagnetism had become a kind of rage by 1850. Electricians (the title had distinguished connotations, like "nuclear physicist" now) had already unveiled one stunning triumph in the telegraph. Their strange new "fluid" was believed capable of such other miracles as propelling cars, restoring vigor, and reviving the recently deceased. It was with expectation of wonders to come that in 1850 Congress appropriated 30,000 dollars for Professor Charles G. Page to build an electric locomotive, to run to Bladensburg, Maryland, 5½ miles from the capital.

Page, then thirty-nine, was an examiner in the United States Patent Office and lecturer on magnetism. An academic person without engineering or railroad training, he believed that electric "engines" should be patterned on steam engines. He designed several great, gawky mechanisms that used solenoids —hollow magnetic coils—like the cylinders of a

*Thomas Davenport,   blacksmith with an endless curiosity
about electromagnetism, made a model electric car in 1834.*

steam engine. They used iron cores for pistons and
had such standard steam regalia as connecting rods,
walking beams, and flywheels.

To help build his locomotive, Page hired a house
carpenter with no more grounding in railroad design
than he had. Their creation was 15 feet long, 6 feet
wide, and was described by even a sympathetic reporter as "illy proportioned." As it neared completion Page discovered that its machinery was poorly
balanced and that the acid had begun to eat through
the fragile cell walls. But the government's appro-
priation was all gone and Page was 6,000 dollars in
debt. He concluded that salvation lay in nursing the
weakened battery through one public demonstration,
after which he could decently apply to Congress for
more money.

The demonstration, on April 29, 1851, was a thin
triumph, tinged with disaster. Seven passengers
climbed aboard with the professor, and the strange-
looking box slowly ground out of Washington Depot.
A small boy scampering alongside had no difficulty
in keeping up. It impressively climbed a short, steep
grade, silencing pessimistic onlookers who had pre-
dicted immediate failure. At the top several cells collapsed and speed dropped to a creep. Ordering his
passengers to walk alongside to lighten the load, the
professor hastily rearranged the wiring around the

*To Professor Page, steam engines pointed out a path by which
the "electric fluid" could be harnessed. His electromagnetic*
*engines used hollow coils like cylinders, moving cores like
pistons, and a walking beam and flywheel for rotary motion.*

dead cells, which brought the car up to a brisk walking pace.

A mile out of town the locomotive inexplicably began to gain speed. The passengers quickly scrambled aboard. It began to go faster and faster, and everyone cheered and rooted the locomotive on, like a race horse. For several minutes the awkward wooden structure bucketed along at about 19 miles an hour. (They calculated speed by timing the revolutions of the drivers.) Then several more cells ruptured and speed fell off to a crawl. Again Page wired around the cells. Further along on the outbound trip the passengers had to dismount to remove a forgotten handcar from the tracks, to shoo away a cow, and to respike a rail that had sprung loose. Despite these delays, the trip to Bladensburg took only thirty-nine minutes.

But the trip back to Washington was nightmarish. Jouncing over the rough rail joints was too much for the battery, and whole groups of cells split in a kind of stampede. Everyone had to abandon the locomotive until the choking acid fumes blew away. By laborious reconnections, the professor was able to marshal about fifty of the original hundred cells—just enough to inch back to the depot. The trip took a full two hours, with fifteen stops for reconnection or for shooing cows off the track.

Congress coolly rejected Page's request for more money, and the project was abandoned. It seems reasonable now that, with better design and luck, the curious box car might have rolled thrillingly to Bladensburg and back at a steady 19 m.p.h. Though a vindication for the professor, this might not have benefited electric transportation. Primary batteries had basic drawbacks in cost, weight, fragility, and limited power. The key that was lacking was a machine for the mechanical production of current.

The dynamo, the machine that generates electricity, took an oddly long time to be invented. It wasn't until 1870 that a Belgian-born Frenchman named Zenobie Theophile Gramme contrived a really successful one. Driven by water power or steam, his machine generated continuous direct current in lavish amounts. After Gramme, electric lights, power, and transportation became imminent.

Two years later Gramme stumbled on something exciting called "reversibility of function." He had discovered that a dynamo was also a motor—rather a poor one, as it happened, though no one suspected that in 1872. If a dynamo's shaft was turned, it generated current; if it was fed current, its shaft turned. Legend has it that one of Gramme's workmen wired a second dynamo to a running one. When he

went to put the driving belt on the second machine, he was thunderstruck to find that it was already spinning away merrily by itself.

In Germany a celebrated electrician named Werner Siemens was working hard. At the Berlin Industrial Exhibition in 1879 he unveiled the first remotely practical electric locomotive. It consisted of a little 2-horsepower dynamo mounted on its side on a narrow-gauge truck. It was ornamentally covered with polished wood and was operated by a dignified technician who perched astride in the stance of a youngster on a kiddy car. It could move at a reliable 8 m.p.h. along the 350 yards of track laid down for it. Pulling three tiny cars holding six passengers apiece, the little locomotive hauled 80,000 persons during the months the Exhibition was open. There was a bare third rail carrying 150 volts, enough to give a vigorous jolt to any person or horse that touched it. Most adults, it was discovered, could be warned off, but neither children nor animals could be depended on to peruse the warning signs.

So popular was this line that it was speedily fol-

This Daft car offered service in 1887 at Orange, N.J. Note the "troller" that was towed along on two wires overhead.

lowed by other exhibition lines in Frankfort, Dusseldorf, and Brussels. Soon too came the jump to a paying enterprise. On May 16, 1881, a Siemens electric line was opened in Lichterfelde, near Berlin, running a mile and a half from the railroad station to a military academy. It used a roofed car, converted from a horsecar, that could carry twenty-six people. There was one motor (actually a dynamo) under the floor, linked to the axles by a cable drive. Top speed was 11 m.p.h., the municipal speed limit, but Siemens technicians whispered that their car could hit 29 m.p.h. if nobody official was looking.

From the beginning the use of the two rails as current conductors gave trouble. Even though the voltage had been reduced to about 100 in an effort to protect people and horses, citizens complained about getting shocked as they crossed the street. Rainy weather sometimes produced an alarming new pyrotechnic called a "short circuit" that scared passersby and stopped service.

In this country, the first dynamo-driven car was a homely little vehicle built by Edison at Menlo Park in the spring of 1880. Edison was then up to his ears

in the development of the incandescent lamp, and his railroad interests were distinctly secondary. He had a notion, however, that electric railroads might come in handy in places where it wasn't worthwhile to build regular ones.

So a bit over a mile of light track was laid down at Menlo Park, and a narrow-gauge locomotive built. The motor was actually one of Edison's best dynamos, a 10-horsepower job of the kind that Edison's associates called a "long-legged Mary Ann" (apparently because the two long field windings gave it, to a technical eye, a kind of biped look). Edison left most of the details to others in his group; the locomotive wasn't one of his better creations. The motor was chiefly controlled by an all-or-nothing switch; the brakes were simply wooden levers that rubbed against the wheels; current was collected from the two rails; and power was transmitted through a friction drive that shattered irreparably on the first trial and had to be replaced by belts.

Still, the little locomotive, towing a tiny passenger car, could whisk along at speeds up to 40 m.p.h. There was a curvy trestle over a low spot at one place

Siemens' locomotive and cars at the Berlin Exhibition in 1879. This was the first remotely practical electric transportation.

Edison's first electric locomotive, built in 1880.
The levers were wheel brakes, useful when it reached speeds of 40 m.p.h.

Siemens' Lichterfelde line in 1881. The small child at left is apt to get a surprise if he touches the two rails at once.

in the line, and careening along that section could be exciting. Some horsecar executives once visited Menlo Park to see how the new wonder was progressing, and Edison gave them rides at such exhilarating velocity that at a convention years later they were still disputing about who'd been scared the most. One of Edison's colleagues used a wild ride on the electric locomotive to take the shine off a brassy young Britisher that Edison had hired as a secretary. The cocky young man, whose name was Samuel Insull, admitted forty-five years later that "the ride about scared the life out of me."

Though reworked several times, Edison's locomotive never showed much promise for the workaday world. For one thing, using the rails as electrical conductors was impractical on public streets; the only way to keep people and animals from serious shocks would have been to reduce the voltage to a point of marginal usefulness. Another difficulty lay in Edison's attitude. Electric cars at this point didn't need inventing half as much as they needed engineering, and this

was work that sometimes bored Edison. Almost wholly taken up in commercializing his lamp, he seems mainly to have considered the locomotive an interesting toy.

When a grasshopper plague swept Kansas in 1879, it cost a farmer named John C. Henry his land, cattle, and two small stores. Determined to find some insect-proof means of remaking his fortune, he moved to Kansas City, got work as a telegraph operator, and polished up plans for a horseless horsecar he had invented. By the fall of 1884 he had raised enough money for a trial. He had bought a dynamo in Chicago and set it up in a little roadside shed, powered by a steam engine taken from an old threshing machine. From a horse railway he wangled the use of an old mule car and a length of track. To keep the electricity out of reach, he stretched two bare copper wires above the track. On top of them there ran two little wheels or "trollers" towed along by wires running down to the mule car beneath.

Professor Sidney Short's "series system"—an enchantingly unsophisticated belief that all the motors in every car should be connected in series, like bulbs on a Christmas tree—was *hotly debated in the early days. It worked on arc lights; why not on cars? Although Short devised controllers so that all streetcars needn't stop at once, his system didn't win out.*

On the first run neither Henry's backers nor any of the spectators proved willing to accompany him. This was perhaps just as well, for when he turned on the current, the trollers sparked furiously, the wheels spun, and the mule car leaped suddenly forward, soon jumping the track and smashing itself on an embankment. The difficulty was in controlling the motor; it was either not going at all or it was going much too fast for the rough track. On a later trial, with two new prospective investors aboard, Henry again accidentally accelerated the mule car to about 15 m.p.h. Then it derailed, stopping so abruptly that all three men were tossed over the dashboard, landing harmlessly in a hedge.

But John C. Henry was persistent and ingenious. Not knowing how to control speed electrically, he determined to do it mechanically. He rebuilt the car with a clutch and a five-speed gear box, much as future automobiles would use. This was costly and cumbersome, but it did tame the all-or-nothing trait. Four cars were equipped in this fashion, and they gave sporadic, halting passenger service for a few months. Then the little line faltered into bankruptcy and was replaced by a cable road. Henry's was an excellent try, but by the middle eighties electric cars needed more engineering development than an amateur could provide.

Two men named Bentley and Knight (both ex-patent examiners, like Professor Page) were energetically bringing electric cars to Cleveland in 1884, with scarcely any more luck. They proposed to conceal the shocking wires in a slotted conduit beneath the surface, much as the cable roads buried their cables. A "plow"—a thin blade extending down from the car through the slot—was to collect the current. Years later, when the frustrations of 1884 could be viewed in wry perspective, Bentley wrote:

The "plow" originally received that designation from the fact that in one of our earliest schemes the top of the conduit was to be made up of hinged sections that were to be lifted up as the car progressed by a device naturally called a plow. But fortunately this was never attempted in practice.

The "fortunately" meant that they had ample troubles already. Bentley and Knight used a mile-long stretch of horsecar track in East Cleveland. It was laid with thin strap rails, set on partly rotted longitudinal wooden stringers, giving the rails a kind of sinuous wave form. "The light car with its short wheelbase," Bentley reported, "would go bobbing along like a ship at sea. It was necessary to anticipate that a car would jump the track at least once a day."

The motor, originally an arc-light dynamo, was

Bentley and Knight worked hard to make this conduit-fed car a success at Cleveland in 1884, but horses came back on duty.

A later Bentley-Knight line in Pittsburgh did a little better, in part because the conduit gave way to two overhead wires.

Neat but not gaudy, Daft's first locomotive had businesslike looks and such unheard-of wonders as electromagnetic brakes.

hung precariously under the car. It was linked to the wheels by coiled springs used as driving belts. Still in his wry mood, Bentley wrote: "These springs would break with a loud report at the rate of about one an hour, and, until the passengers got used to it, there was a serious commotion each time it occurred."

Troubles were endless. The conduit was constructed of wood, and boards kept springing loose and fouling the plow. Each derailment meant that the plow was destructively jerked from the slot, ripping the conduit in pieces. When the plow was made slim enough to permit nondestructive derailments, it developed a tendency to break off in ordinary use. One very old gentleman, a director of the company and thus entitled to special attention, kept showing up at the scene to demand assurance that electricity *really* could travel rapidly enough to keep up with the car, a concept that was a constant source of wonder to him. When rain and snow came in the fall of 1884, difficulties began to multiply. Sometimes a car would give a measure of service for as much as a week, but then repairs would bring a long interruption. The experiment was abandoned that winter and horses took over once more.

By a kind of natural selection, the dream of electric cars came most vividly to exceptional men, and among these Leo Daft was one of the most unusual.

Born in England in 1843, he was the son of an engineer who worked on early iron bridges and ships. His adolescence was spent in fascinated tinkering with daguerreotypes and telegraphs. He worked for a time as a draftsman for his father but found civil engineering dreary in comparison with the new excitements of photography and electricity. He left home at twenty-three and came to the United States and in the seventies started a photo studio in Troy, New York. A hard-working and clever young man, Daft produced a spectacular 7-foot panoramic photograph of the Mohawk Valley and sold the first print for 300 dollars. Being a person whose interest dulled as soon as an activity threatened to become easy and commercial, Daft soon turned to electricity, where he encountered enough difficulties to keep him interested most of his life.

By 1882 he had a little electric-light company at work in a New Jersey town. One day he experimentally mounted a motor on wheels, trying it on a little track at the factory grounds. It had remarkable traction—the 450-pound locomotive could exert a 300-pound pull on dry rails—and Daft theorized that the flow of current between rails and wheels somehow increased adhesion. Knowing that driver-slippage was a continuing headache with steam locomotives, where there was plenty of power but rarely enough traction, Daft was suddenly caught up in a glowing vision of an all-conquering electric locomotive. Initially committed by this motion to the use of the rails as one of the current conductors, he resolved to eliminate shocks by using very low voltages—maybe just 20 or 25 volts.

Clearly the first step was to raise capital, and for this a demonstration was needed. In May of 1883 he began to build a working locomotive, the *Ampère,* named, it was explained, "after the famous French electrician." It weighed 2 tons, had a 25-horsepower motor, and drew current from a third rail, returning it via the running rails. Its speed could be controlled electrically. Daft arranged for a trial on a 1¼-mile stretch of the Saratoga and Mt. McGregor Railway, a narrow-gauge scenic line that meandered out from the New York State resort. Working with appalling energy (all the early experimenters seem to have been virtually inexhaustible) he installed a steam engine and boiler to run the dynamo, laid his third rail on its wooden insulators, borrowed a regular passenger car for the *Ampère* to tow, and invited an array of bankers, lawyers, businessmen, and newspaper reporters to watch the trial.

Like Professor Page's Bladensburg trip, the demonstration on November 24, 1883, was a kind of Pyrrhic triumph. After the distinguished visitors had inspected the *Ampère,* Daft ran it up and down the track, pointing out how it moved smoothly and cleanly in silence. Then the passenger car was hooked on and everyone was invited to climb aboard and observe the engine's pulling power. About sixty persons boarded the car and, with Daft at the controls of the *Ampère,* were drawn smoothly out to the end of the electrified section. Everyone marveled at how the little locomotive capably hauled its 16-ton load along a winding, uphill track at an impressive 8 m.p.h. But on the downhill trip Daft enthusiastically accelerated to 15 m.p.h., and on a sharp curve the *Ampère* left the rails and toppled over with a resounding crash. The *Ampère* was wrecked, but neither Daft, who had been pitched into a providential sandbank, nor any of the dignitaries aboard the car were seriously hurt. Dazed, Daft is said to have stood staring at the smashed locomotive and repeating, "We *were* going too fast." The whole party limped disconsolately back to the station, ignoring sardonic comments from the steam-locomotive crew dispatched to haul in the pieces.

Daft appears to have thrived on difficulty. He bounced back in a few months with two new locomotives, the *Volta* and the *Pacinotti,* that were operated as scientific novelties in Boston and at the Iron Pier on Coney Island, where they provided the public with the thrill of "electrical rides." It was at Coney Island that a vacationer named Thomas Robbins saw the little cars and became highly impressed. Robbins, general manager of a Baltimore horsecar system, had one curvy, hilly branch line that was a horse killer. Could Mr. Daft's little machines handle it? He was enthusiastically assured that they could.

But in Baltimore Robbins' board of directors were lukewarm. They consulted a scientist and were told that "the man who undertakes to operate this section by electricity in the present state of the art is either a knave or a fool." At this the directors flatly vetoed the whole notion. His judgment questioned, Robbins delivered an angry ultimatum: either the directors would give Daft a chance or Robbins himself would quit. Since Robbins was an unusually able manager, the directors agreed to what they called a compromise—Daft could electrify the branch and provide locomotives at his own expense. If they delivered entirely satisfactory service for a full year, the directors would buy the equipment. It was a singularly unfair contract, but Daft jumped at the chance.

The 3-mile line was another partial success—the first regularly operated electric line in America that kept going for an appreciable time. It opened for a

The "Ampère" just before it was wrecked. It is possible that the alert electrician at the controls above was Daft himself.

Leo Daft leans against his locomotive at Baltimore in 1885.

secret trial on August 9, 1885 (at one in the morning, in case of embarrassments) and began regular passenger service the next day. The alert and apprehensive passengers rode in their regular horsecars, but in place of the familiar team out front there were boxy little locomotives that were labeled the *Morse,* the *Faraday,* or the *Ohm.* To the end of his life Daft never missed a chance to recount gleefully how the scientist who had inferentially called him a fool or knave had been whisked along the Hampden branch at double a horsecar's speed and had had to pay a fare for the privilege. A year after opening the branch was still giving moderately satisfactory service, and Daft was reimbursed.

There were continuing difficulties, however, mainly centering on the third rail. Heavy rains often caused short circuits that brought everything to a halt. To keep the cars from slowing down away from the powerhouse, it proved necessary to use about 120 volts—five times the amount Daft had hoped—and this led to continuing shock complaints. In wet weather, dogs, cats, and chickens were sometimes electrocuted. Stepping on the third rail did not appear to injure horses, though it did stimulate giddier ones into running away. After a few shocks, staid and older horses either refused to cross the tracks or else learned to step fastidiously over the rails—habits that they solemnly followed long after electrification was abandoned.

Where the tracks were at roadside or on a private right-of-way these problems were comparatively minor. But at major street crossings so much public hostility (and so many lawsuits) developed that the company was forced to remove the third rail, replacing it at the crossings with lengths of gas pipe suspended over the tracks like trolley wire. When the "engineer" trundled up to a crossing, he was a fran-

tically busy fellow: his right hand stayed on the brake handle, its slack wound up; his left hand first set the controller at a low-speed notch and then immediately worked a long lever that erected a pole, ending in iron fingers, up against the gas pipe overhead; one foot pumped a pedal that raised up the third-rail contact wheel; and then, as soon as practicable, his other foot clanged a warning gong.

How Daft felt when the Hampden branch was ignominiously turned back to horses is not known, but it seems likely that he was too busy with his newest enthusiasm to grieve long. This was the *Benjamin Franklin,* the biggest locomotive yet, built for experimental use on the Ninth Avenue Elevated in New York City, which was then operated by capable but dirty steam locomotives. *Benjamin* weighed almost 9 tons and was initially disappointing. Rebuilt in 1888, it did much better, pulling eight-car passenger trains at speeds up to 25 m.p.h.

In the late eighties Daft turned back to street transportation, installing "Daft System" lines in several Connecticut cities and in Orange and Asbury Park, New Jersey. Unlike his previous efforts these involved electrified horsecars rather than separate locomotives. The low-voltage third rail was abandoned in favor of two overhead wires, on which there rode grooved-wheel trollers. Daft had continuing bad luck with the trollers, which toppled off the wires with distressing frequency.

By the end of the decade, when superior designs were steadily taking over, a body of folklore sprang up about Daft cars—much as thirty years later similar, affectionately derisive tales would cluster around the Ford flivver. One story told of a newly hired conductor who doggedly climbed up on the roof of his car five times, each time being flung off by the shock as he awkwardly tried to replace the troller. Finally he managed to set it correctly in place, but the

A pole was hoisted when the third rail stopped at crossings.

A cog wheel on the locomotive and a rack in the center of the track were thought to make this Pittsburgh car safe on hills.

Built to replace steam on the Elevated in New York, Daft's "Benjamin Franklin" was a disappointment until rebuilt later.

Sparking and humming, Daft cars appeared in Asbury Park, N.J., in 1887. One difficulty of many with overhead trollers was persuading them to follow along docilely at a switch.

car hadn't traveled for more than a block before it fell off again, whereupon he unprintably resigned and retired to a bar. Then there was the Daft line that achieved a measure of reliability by hiring small boys, fitting them with rubber gloves, and keeping them on the car roofs as troller restorers. And then there was the incident which caused Daft cars to be permanently barred in one Connecticut city. After many complaints about the service, the mayor assigned a city official to investigate. This worthy promptly left the meeting, stepped into the street, and signaled for a Daft car to stop. When it did the troller coasted on ahead as usual until pulled up short by the wires—too short, for it fell off and struck the official squarely on the head, sending him to the hospital for six weeks.

Leo Daft lived to be seventy-nine. He died in 1922, at the height of the trolley era he worked so hard to start.

One of the first electric cars in Canada, this one ran in Ontario about 1888. Its motor, on the front platform, drove the front wheels by a chain. Two retractable brooms could be lowered to sweep the track bare ahead of the wheels.

Another almost-successful pioneer was Charles J. Van Depoele, Daft's closest rival. Born in Belgium in 1846, he built a telegraph at ten, speedily developed a facility in eight languages, and was deeply preoccupied with what was then termed "natural philosophy." There were family anxieties over this one-sidedness, and his father apprenticed him at sixteen to a religious wood carver in Paris.

Van Depoele stuck it out long enough to become an expert cabinetmaker and then, with the assistance of a sympathetic aunt, ran away to America. He came to Detroit, set up as a wood carver, and was almost immediately successful. By twenty-three he was the proprietor of a woodworking shop employing several hundred people. Like Daft, Van Depoele found it difficult to remain interested in a commercially successful enterprise. He brought his family to this country, turned the shop over to his father, and announced he was going to concentrate on electricity.

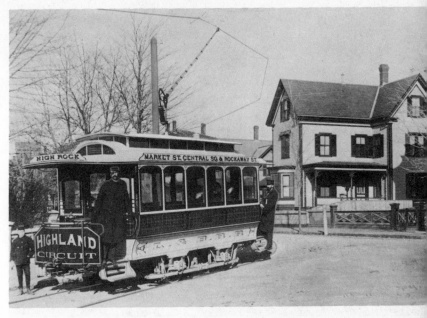

Electric transportation came to Lynn, Mass., with this improved Van Depoele car that sported a spring-raised trolley.

Charles Van Depoele's cars came to the edge of practicality.

He formed an electric arc-light company in Chicago and in 1878 showed a flair for promotion by using his arcs to illuminate the "great tent" of the Forepaugh Circus. By 1882 he was hard at work experimenting with electric cars. (One of the experiments—which turned out to be important in a later patent fight—involved a single overhead wire, with an underrunning trolley wheel pressed up against it. It seemed mildly promising, but then so did various other methods.) By the fall of 1883 he had a tiny show car ready for the Chicago Industrial Exposition. It seems to have drawn its current from a wire in a trough between the tracks.

Van Depoele apparently realized, like Siemens in Berlin, that a fair or exposition was a perfect location for electric cars. Here were masses of people, a captive audience ready to be impressed; their feet would be throbbingly grateful for even a short ride; and the operating environment was much less harsh than in the rough, tough horsecar world. In 1884 he unveiled another little show line, also conduit fed, at the Toronto Exposition. The following year he was back in Toronto with an enlarged version. It proved to be a stunning success.

The track ran about a mile from a railroad station to within the Exposition grounds. Van Depoele used one motor car, capable of hauling three trailers. It could hit 30 m.p.h. and had no difficulty in making the round trip in seven or eight minutes. Once it carried 50,000 passengers in a five-day period. Van Depoele had no truck with Daft's low-voltage theories

Towing trailer-loads of people at brisk speeds, Van Depoele's trolley at the 1885 Toronto Exposition was a hit of the show.

His installation at Montgomery, Ala., was Van Depoele's most ambitious one. The cars ultimately used trolley poles.

and rather casually reported that he found it "expedient to use an electro motive force of about 1,400 volts and an intensity of about 18 ampères." (It seems fortunate that he didn't share Daft's early preference for electrified rails, since this voltage could have stacked up the corpses like cordwood. What made both the lethal voltage and the good service possible was the fact that he was using a trolley pole ending in an underrunning wheel.)

Van Depoele did not realize immediately what an excellent gadget the trolley pole was. In his first commercial street line, opened in South Bend later in 1885, he used a little troller dragged along overhead. Similar troublemakers were used by subsequent Van Depoele lines in Scranton, Pennsylvania, Appleton, Wisconsin, and elsewhere. He preferred, however, to call them "travelers." In Scranton a sign was posted in the station reading "Engineers must oil their travelers every three hours." This provoked the *Scranton Republican* to the comment that "To set minds at rest, it may be well to state that 'travelers' has no reference to passengers riding in the cars but only to the little arrangement that runs on the wire above."

Van Depoele and Daft disagreed sharply as to where a streetcar motor should be located, Van Depoele favoring the front platform and Daft preferring a position underneath. Some unknown reproach stung the Van Depoele camp into a tart letter to the *Street Railway Journal* in 1887: "Motors underneath were tried by us *years* ago. There were very many *serious* objections. It is easy to run an electric railroad on *paper*. . . ." The dispute promptly moved over to public advertisements: Daft passengers were assured that their watches would never become magnetized in Daft cars, and Van Depoele riders learned that: "As the motor is placed upon the front platform of the car, it is at all times under the eyes of the driver. This enables him to take good care of the machine, and to see that all working parts are in good order. From this point he can also attend to the oiling of the shafts."

Van Depoele cars achieved a precarious foothold in four or five cities by 1886. Whenever possible the powerhouse dynamo was driven by water power rather than by a steam engine, and it was at first the economical practice to leave the plant running unattended. But some costly accidents when waterwheel governors stuck open, overspeeding the dynamos and generating fearsome voltages before the machinery smashed, put a stop to this parsimony. In his most ambitious early installation, in Montgomery, Alabama, in 1886, Van Depoele went back to the use of a trolley. This appears to have been the one part of the equipment that was fairly satisfactory.

Little else was. It turned out that the overhanging front platforms weren't really strong enough to support the heavy motors; after running on rough track for a few weeks, the whole structure of the little horsecars would begin to break up. Motors themselves gave continuing trouble—sparking so badly under their primitive metal brushes that they could run only a few hours between overhauls. The drive system gave frequent headaches; "dirt lodged in cog wheel" was a frequent cause of interruptions.

A whole new family of difficulties arose whenever the running rails were used as the return half of the electrical circuit. This was because no one realized how important it was for the rail joints to be bonded into excellent electrical connections. Where the joints were loose—which, at first, was almost everywhere—the current would seek a better underground route back to the powerhouse. The favorite route was via

Cutaway view of a Van Depoele car as used in Scranton, Pa. In the view of its builder, a motor needed continual scrutiny.

This Van Depoele car began operating in Lima, Ohio, in 1887, and was thus one of the earliest U.S. electric cars in com- *mercial use. But the unreliability of the motor and its chain drive handicapped the cars in competing with perfected mules.*

buried water and gas pipes, and these promptly began to corrode electrolytically. Before long a rash of unexpected pipe burstings impaired still further the shaky reputation of electric cars. There was a related difficulty with telephones, which at that time used the ground as part of *their* circuitry. As a result the telephones transmitted only an impenetrable hiss whenever an electric car was in operation.

Elmer Morris, Van Depoele's chief assistant, once confided his technique for coping with the current leakages that brought these troubles. Standing on the rear platform of a moving car, he'd watch the track closely. Whenever he saw the flash of an arc spluttering at the rail joint, he'd hop off and hammer in a spike between the rail ends. "Of course," he admitted wearily, "the spike would work out in a few days and I'd have to do it again." Incidentally, Morris, though invaluable to Van Depoele, was able to draw only

ninety-five dollars in salary for one eleven-month stretch and was so hard up when they won a contract in Ansonia, Connecticut, that he had to walk there.

By the beginning of 1887, electric cars were an accomplished if faltering fact in America, though they hadn't even begun to threaten the enormous horse and cable roads in the big cities. There were ten intermittently running installations, about 60 miles of track, and less than one hundred electric cars. The equipment was highly various: high voltage and low; third rails, conduits, trolleys, and trollers; motors were located on and under cars, driving by chains, belts, and gears. Yet all lines had one thing in common—a maddening unwillingness to work right for any length of time. Such was the situation when an extraordinarily self-assured young man turned up, to change the face of virtually every city and town in the land.

The crank on top of a Van Depoele motor established how fast it went; the two levers at the side controlled the way it went and how badly it sparked while doing it. There was a position of "minimum sparking" for each speed. Wheeling, W.Va., in 1887.

6. FRANK SPRAGUE BUILDS A TROLLEY

> *. . . 500 volts is the highest that Mr. Sprague allows, because more would be apt to cause serious personal inconvenience in case of touching the conductors.*
>
> —*Description of early streetcar*

Except for one reason, Frank Julian Sprague's name might be as familiar today as that of Thomas Alva Edison or Alexander Graham Bell. Many of Sprague's electrical patents were basic. Most of his inventions were beautifully engineered—they generally *wanted* to work, not to act up. And he fathered not only the first practical, city-wide trolley system, but also modern subway and elevated trains, automatic train-safety controls, and the high-speed electric elevators without which tall city buildings would be impractical. The reason why his name is little known today is that, on many of the occasions when he sold his patents to General Electric, Westinghouse, Otis Elevator, and other firms, he did not insist that his name be identified with the products he had made possible. (At first he simply assumed that his name would be retained and was hurt that it wasn't.) Much of the early fame that such companies won was earned for them by Frank Sprague's brain.

Sprague was both an authentic genius and an engaging person, self-assured, but so calm about it that he never seemed cocky. He was born in Connecticut in 1857 and at sixteen, a mathematical wizard, entered the class of 1878 at Annapolis. His classmates found Sprague to be a skinny youngster who, in any physical dispute, could usually be knocked down but who had a tireless tendency to bounce up fighting. Graduating with high honors, he sailed on a cruise to the Far East on the U.S.S. *Richmond*. It was no pleasure junket for Sprague; he stepped ashore afterward with preliminary applications drawn for almost sixty electrical patents, thought up on his off-duty shipboard hours.

Assigned to the Torpedo Station at Newport, Rhode Island, the young midshipman there met Professor Moses Farmer, then "government electrician" for the station. This was the same man who had built a little battery-powered car thirty-three years earlier.

Sprague, then full of cloudy plans for revolutionizing the dynamo, had his mind directed for a moment by the old professor to the idea of electric transportation. At any rate, he tossed off a basic invention for the speed control of electric motors—a concept simultaneously announced by a distinguished British scientist—and then went back to re-engineering dynamos. But Farmer's idea was planted.

In 1882 Sprague wangled a three months' leave of absence at his own expense so that he could attend the Crystal Palace Exhibition in London. When he returned to this country in May of the following year, the Navy was grim: he had overstayed his orders by some six months and a court-martial was docketed. It never came to trial, however, for Sprague produced an explanation that was entirely in character—a dazzling 169-page technical report on all electrical apparatus shown at the Exhibition, including charts, circuit drawings, and detailed performance tests. It turned out that the young ensign, far from having merely gone AWOL, had managed to get himself appointed secretary of the Exhibition's scientific jury and thus had a fine chance to examine and test all the newest electrical devices shown. The Navy published his report and canceled the court-martial.

At some point during his stay in London, Sprague directed his restless mind toward the idea of electric transportation. Years later he said it happened on his daily trips to the London tubes, which were then operated by coal-burning locomotives, almost asphyxiating their riders. He conceived of a trolley, a "self-adjusting, upward-pressure contact," but did not apply for a patent until three years later, which was a mistake. Writing forty-nine years afterward, in the Patent Office prose he sometimes used, Sprague stated:

About the same time, but I think later, the idea of a trailing trolley occurred to Charles Van Depoele in the

Frank J. Sprague at the time he was building his trolleys.

around him a number of assistants who, like himself, instinctively distrusted academic training and highly prized a let's-try-it-and-see-what-happens approach. The Menlo Park viewpoint sometimes edged toward derision of training; they liked to chuckle about the time a college graduate had been told to find the volume of a new shape of light bulb, and the poor lad had plunged into days of fruitless calculation—until Edison told him to fill the bulb with water and see how much it held.

Sprague on his side was baffled by this cult of empiricism. Fresh from a fine technical school, he was highly trained in mathematics and engineering, and he could see no handicap in this. The issue arose when he discovered with astonishment how the Edison company was determining what size of wires to use in a new lighting system. A huge map of the community to be electrified was laid out on a panel. At each house where electricity was subscribed for, a peg was inserted. On this peg was put a spool of resistance wire, with turns in proportion to the number of lights ordered for that house. Then little, scaled-down feeder wires were run along the model streets and the whole distribution system was built in miniature. When it was done—it took weeks—its electrical characteristics were measured, scaled up to full size, and the right wires thus determined.

All this flabbergasted Sprague. He pulled out a pencil, speedily devised a formula for determining wire sizes, and then tactfully explained that the answer could be obtained far more quickly, cheaply, and accurately by calculation than by model-making. The Edison company seems to have had some initial suspicion of this bookish approach. But it worked beautifully, so the company adopted it, as all generating systems soon did.

Sprague spent less than a year with Edison. Once, in Sunbury, Pennsylvania, he forgot to oil a new dynamo and its bearings burned out, amid general consternation, on the final trial the evening before the new plant was to be ceremoniously opened. Edison, Sprague, and a machinist worked irritably all night long to fit new bearings; and Sprague seems to have been lubrication-sensitive for years. Later in 1883, installing the first electric lights in Brockton, Massachusetts, Sprague spent his spare time dreaming of the possibilities of electric motors for transportation. In a little machine shop down the street he made a working model of his first railroad motor.

In the spring of 1884 Sprague took the plunge. He quit his job and formed his own company, the Sprague Electric Railway & Motor Company. It had practically no capital—a wisp of savings and a couple of shares sold to friends, all of which promptly dis-

United States, and when some years later we both began to use it, a patent interference resulted. In its conduct all evidence of my conception was declared inadmissible except as of date of reentrance into the United States, in May of 1883, despite my actual presence for part of the time as an officer on an American man-of-war, and hence on American soil. The United States dates slightly favored Van Depoele, and a patent was finally issued to him, but with arrangements made for mutual use.

Resigning from the Navy, Sprague went to work for Edison at Menlo Park. It's possible that one attraction there was the little Edison locomotive, then being rebuilt for the third time, in collaboration with Stephen Field. If so, it would have been chiefly interesting to Sprague as a collection of characteristics to be avoided; he shrugged it off as "having little if any novelty," and Edison promptly assigned him to the job of helping install new electric-light systems.

Neither the Menlo Park group nor Sprague knew quite what to make of the other. Edison had gathered

appeared in living expenses. To carry on, Sprague made a deal with E. H. Johnson, a businessman associated with Edison, in which Johnson would progressively advance small cash sums in return for increasing interests in the company. (This proved a jackpot for Johnson; in three years he sold his Sprague shares for 400,000 dollars to the Edison General Electric Company and blew himself to an elegant chateau in Connecticut that had once belonged to Andrew Carnegie.) Meanwhile Sprague, allotting himself a salary of 2,500 dollars a year, was building his first electric motors.

They were startlingly good. First shown in the fall of 1884 at a Philadelphia exposition, they immediately won attention because they weren't just dynamos used reversibly. Sprague had designed motors *as* motors, with greatly improved performance. Soon orders were coming in from all over the United States and from Europe. And Edison endorsed them as the only motors recommended for use on his lighting systems. Sprague's little company grew strong and

healthy, and its young founder turned his full attention toward electric railroads.

On East 24th Street in New York City, at the Durant Sugar Refinery, there was a 200-foot length of track in an alley between two buildings. Early in 1886 Sprague managed to get the use of it for experimenting on the electric car that he hoped might soon replace steam on the Elevateds. At first he used an ordinary railroad flatcar, wholly unprepossessing. Underneath, however, were ideas that soon were to win worldwide use. There were two gear-drive motors in one truck, ingeniously mounted in what Sprague called "wheelbarrow fashion." Part of the motor was supported around the axle, and part was spring-mounted on the truck frame. Thus the motor could bounce on bumps, but only in an arc about the axle that carefully preserved gear spacing. It was an idea of such engineering sophistication as to make the designs of Edison, Daft, and Van Depoele seem like cave drawings.

There were other bright ideas too: highly efficient

His Richmond cars were the first to be really successful.

motors, flexible control, and something called regenerative braking. This was an idea that had been kicking around for some time but had never been adequately developed—the motors were employed as generators during braking, slowing the car down and sometimes even pumping electricity back into the system.

Although the flatcar behaved well, Sprague muffed his first big chance. He staged a demonstration before a group of railroad owners and financiers headed by Jay Gould. Sprague wanted desperately to impress the assemblage with the ease with which the car could be controlled on so short a length of track. He enticed Gould aboard the car, stationing him at the front by the controller. Close to where Gould was standing was the main fuse, an open bit of lead wire in the motor circuit. To show off acceleration, Sprague cranked the controller around too fast, and the open fuse blew with a bright yellow flash and a loud report. To everyone's alarm, Gould tried to jump off the car. (It was probably this momentary panic in front of his colleagues that, in retrospect, upset the financier the most.) Sprague said later that "my explanation that this young volcano was really only a safety device was not convincing, and Gould did not return." Sprague cars were successfully demonstrated on the Manhattan Elevated later that year, but the line's directors were noticeably cool. Considering Jay

Gould's eminence, it seems possible that the blown fuse may have delayed rail electrification in the United States by several years.

Sprague bounced back from this absurd defeat to one of the greatest triumphs of his life. In May, 1887, he signed a contract to provide a complete electrical street-railway system for Richmond, Virginia. It was a big contract, hardly a prudent venture for an under-capitalized twenty-nine-year-old to tackle. As he wrote later:

It called for the completion in ninety days of the equipment of a road having about twelve miles of track, at that time unlaid, and with the route only provisionally determined; the construction of a complete steam and electric central-station plant of 375-hp. capacity; and the furnishing of forty cars with eighty motors and all appurtenances necessary to their operation. This was nearly as many motors as there were in use on all the cars throughout the rest of the world. Thirty cars were to be operated at one time, and grades as steep as 8 percent were to be mounted. Finally, the payment was to be $110,000, "if satisfactory."

At the time the contract was signed, Sprague's company had on hand only a blueprint of a proposed streetcar and some experimental equipment left over from the elevated venture. Almost immediately, in the classic early streetcar tradition, matters began to go wrong. Exhausted by overwork, Sprague caught

Before Sprague, electric-car inventors faced a thorny dilemma: if the heavy motors were not spring-mounted, they might be shaken to pieces; if they were, gear mesh was not reliable. His "wheelbarrow" mounting proved the answer.

typhoid fever and was out of action for weeks. In his absence, many initial decisions had to be taken by his two even younger assistants. Both of them, by no coincidence, were freshly graduated from the service academies. Ensign S. Dana Greene took over in Richmond, and Lt. Oscar T. Crosby, newly from West Point, held the fort in New York, where the equipment was manufactured. When after nine weeks Sprague came shakily back to work, much of the track had been laid and some of the motors built.

The track was laid by an independent contractor. It was, Sprague found, "simply execrable, built for profit, not for permanence. The rail was of antiquated shape, poorly jointed, unevenly laid, insecurely tied; the foundation was red clay. Many curves were sharp, and the rail spread easily. One grade, nearly a mile long, was in places nearly 10 percent."

When limited trials on part of the track began, it grew evident that the two 7-horsepower motors on each car were none too powerful for their task. Often a loaded car would stick on a hilly curve, and Sprague fell into the habit of stationing three or four husky employees on the rear platform. They had standing instructions to jump off and push whenever the car threatened to stall—an assignment soon known as "playing the mule." If a car expired away from the carbarn (many did, at first) real mules were sent out after dark to drag it home.

By the time the track was finished and the overhead wire was strung, everyone was doubtful as to whether the motors with their single reduction gears would be able to manage the steeper grades. Sprague thought that by straining them slightly they could have made the somewhat gentler slopes originally contracted for. But both he and Greene had increasing misgivings. They decided to change to a double reduction gear for each motor—though this would entail tricky modification of the ones already built and delays in manufacture of the rest. Then the alarming thought struck them that even this might not be enough. It would give the motors ample torque, but suppose the grades were beyond the limits of wheel-to-track adhesion?

Desperately, they began to doodle out an auxiliary cable scheme. Electric motors would be set beneath the tracks, pulling endless cables that would boost the cars up the toughest spots. E. H. Johnson, the businessman who had been advancing Sprague installments of working capital, was present in Richmond at the evening conference when this dismaying possibility came up. Unenthusiastic over the ease with which these bright youngsters could invent costly solutions, he said: "Guess the first thing is to find out

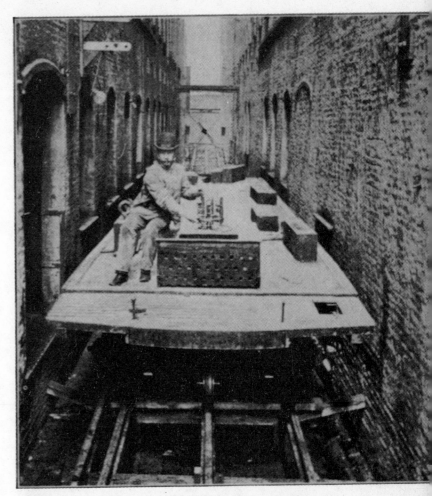

It was on the 200 feet of track in this alley that a scare from a blown fuse eliminated Jay Gould as a Sprague backer.

if the car can get up the grade by itself." So at nine that night in November, 1887, the conference adjourned to a trolley car to try it on the worst hill. Wrote Sprague:

If we succeeded in climbing the hill I knew what would probably happen to the machines; but it was vital to learn whether a self-propelled car could be made to go up that grade at all. We went steadily up that and another hill, around several curves, and finally reached the highest point of the line in the heart of the city. I knew that the motors must be pretty hot.

An enthusiastic crowd soon gathered [a theater had just let out] and in the delay I was in hopes that the motors would cool down sufficiently to permit us to continue the journey. No sooner, however, had we started than I felt a peculiar bucking movement, and knew that we were disabled. The trouble was due to a crossed [short-circuited] armature, then a little-known difficulty.

Unwilling to admit serious trouble, I told Greene, in a tone that could be overheard, that there was some slight trouble in the circuits, and he would better go for

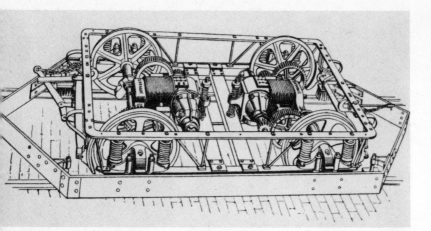

This is what moved the world's first practical trolleys. The truck shown is one having the extra stage of gear reduction.

Ten per cent grades and inferior track multiplied the difficulties. The photograph shows a stretch in Richmond in 1888.

the instruments so that we could locate it. Then turning out the lights, I lay down on a seat to wait, while the crowd gradually dispersed. After waiting a long time for Greene's return with those "instruments," inwardly praying that he would be late, he came in sight with four of them, big, powerful mules, the most effective aids which could be found in Richmond under the circumstances.

The knowledge that the hills *could* be climbed was cheering, and Sprague hastened to build in the extra gears that would ease the load on the motors. But other problems descended in a steady rain. Track switches and the accompanying divisions in the overhead wire were severe headaches at first. Sprague originally tried to use a vertical trolley pole, which proved unsatisfactory. Forty different designs were built and tried out, and thirty-nine of them did poorly. The fortieth, suggested by a draftsman named Eugene Pommer, consisted of a trailing inclined pole, freely pivoted and pressed upward by springs. It worked fine and had the additional merit of being easily reversible at the end of the line.

The construction syndicate in Richmond, which was fighting off bankruptcy, put pressure on Sprague for an immediate start to commercial operations. Unwilling to begin until he had a chance of delivering, Sprague insisted on a series of postponements which inevitably resulted in mutual recriminations and suspended payments. By late January, 1888, opening could be postponed no longer without risk of well-publicized failure. Ten cars had been brought to a state where it seemed they might work for a time. Wrote Sprague:

As a preliminary to regular operation, we spent a day carrying loads of children without any serious trouble, and about the 2nd of February, 1888, in a drizzling rain we opened the line for regular service.

The day was one of disappointment; we carried crowds of people, but car after car would suddenly stop in the street and refuse to move under any conditions, for the new gears had a freak of locking. The men got under the cars, took off the disgruntled gears, and continued, if possible, on the other machine, or bodily hauled the car off the track so that another could go by.

My first impression was that it was a mechanical fault, that the gears were not properly cut or that the castings had been distorted. But an Irish mechanic, Pat O'Shaughnessy, who had been with me for years, and who had a most happy mechanical judgment, insisted that it was for lack of proper oiling, and after a while had the cars running again.

This same happy judgment helped out again not long after. Sprague had worked late one night and overslept the following morning. When he awoke in his rooming house on the car line, he saw that sleety

were supposed to be interchangeable but usually weren't until they were laboriously cobbled in the carbarn. Never one for wild talk, Sprague said, "Greene, this is hell."

Motor brushes—the contacts that pressed against the spinning commutator—were endlessly troublesome. Then made of metal, they sparked destructively, arcing and sputtering and welding themselves into worthlessness. Sprague spent weeks in experimenting with brush design. Sometimes he achieved a little improvement in performance, usually at a penalty elsewhere:

After a Richmond derailment, riders and passers-by usually found a sturdy pole and helped lever the car onto the rails.

rain had fallen during the night, coating the trolley wire with an icy insulation. Prospective passengers had collected at the car stops but no cars were running. Then, as he watched, one car appeared around the bend, making its way slowly but steadily and followed by several others that picked up passengers. Braced on top of the first car, continuously thwacking the ice off the wire with an upended broom, was the intrepid Pat O'Shaughnessy.

For months it was an enormous struggle to keep the cars running. Troubles with the motors were endless. Windings kept short-circuiting and burning out, and many parts had to be shipped back to New York for rebuilding. Soon a continuous flow of burned out and rewired parts, traveling expensively by express, sprang up between Richmond and New York. For a time Sprague and Greene lived in constant fear that it would prove impossible to provide new motors as fast as the ones in use failed. Parts

Pat O'Shaughnessy, one of Sprague's master mechanics rode on top with a broom to open the line after an ice storm.

The track soon looked like a golden path, for the rough commutator bars acted like a milling cutter and sheared off the ends of the [brushes] with marvelous rapidity, sending a shower of shimmering scales over machines and roadway. At this period we were using about $9 worth of brass per day for brushes; not half a trip was made without inspection and generally a change of brushes.

Then gradually, almost imperceptibly, things began to get better. Sprague and Greene noticed that although new difficulties kept cropping up in a steady parade, they weren't as mean and obdurate as earlier problems. Cars available for service in the spring of 1888 gradually increased to twenty, thirty, and finally and intoxicatingly, to forty. Just as Sprague had calculated, the power plant proved capable of handling thirty cars at once as a "distributed load" and he admitted to relief from secret anxieties when his figures checked out. Each motor was progressively rewound in a way that produced less sparking and few short circuits. Richmond telephones—which had initially transmitted only "hissing and frying" whenever the cars were running—came clear again after the telephone superintendent gave up and surrendered the earth to Sprague, installing wire returns on all phone circuits.

The original operating syndicate in Richmond had gone bankrupt shortly after the opening. The receivers took over and carried on, but Sprague suffered a heavy financial loss. He estimated that his company spent 75,000 dollars more than it was paid. Before long it became evident, however, that this immediate deficit was more than made up for by the technical experience and the national reputation the company gained. Horsecar and cable executives from many parts of the country made pilgrimages to Richmond to study the exciting new system. By the summer of 1888 so many new installations were in sight that it became apparent that Sprague's little cars heralded the start of a whole new industry.

Among the most prominent of the visitors was an impressive gentleman named Henry M. Whitney, president of the West End Railroad in Boston. This was a large and prosperous line—several thousand horses worked for Mr. Whitney—that was about ready to convert to power. The general manager, a man named Longstreet, strongly favored a cable-car system. Whitney felt that prudence required at least a look at this electrical idea. They went first to Alleghany City, Pennsylvania, where a small Bentley-Knight line was under way. Whitney was impressed, though Longstreet wasn't, and they traveled down to Richmond. Aware that this was the first nibble from a big-city system, Sprague pulled out all the stops to

Once the line's worst troubles were past, the city grew fond of its Richmond Union Passenger Railway. It was then the only large trolley-car system in the world, and street-railway magnates made pilgrimages just to study it. Riding on the new cars was both exciting and fashionable—just the thing, as above, to finish off a cultural evening in the theater.

impress the visitors. It became evident that the stumbling block was Longstreet. Electric cars would never do in big cities, he contended, because an inevitable traffic snarl would bunch a string of cars together on a single line. When the congestion cleared, all waiting cars would try to start up at once, creating a sudden load that would destroy the dynamos.

This piece of ingenious pessimism had Whitney wavering. Sprague privately resolved to stage a demonstration of "somewhat dramatic character." One night after service shut down, he collected twenty-two cars and "banked" them—parked them virtually touching at one end of the line. He ordered the central-station engineer to keep the fires hot and build up all the steam the boilers could carry. Telling the engineer to wire extra fuses in parallel on the mains, he instructed him to "keep going no matter what."

It was midnight when all was ready. Sprague sent an invitation to Whitney, who'd gone to bed, to come see an experimental test of Longstreet's gloomy notion. When the visitors arrived, Sprague explained that the section the cars were parked on was designed to power only four well-spaced cars at one time. Then

he waved a signal lantern and the motormen of the twenty-two cars started up, each one pulling away as soon as he had a few feet of headway. The electrical drain was plainly severe, and lamps in the cars dimmed down progressively to a barely visible orange glow. (At the powerhouse, the steam engines labored to keep going, and trolley voltage dropped from 500 to less than 200 volts.) Still, to Sprague's delight, "every car got away and soon was bustling out of sight."

The stunt pushed Whitney off the fence. Back in Boston he delivered a glowing eulogy of electric cars in applying to the Aldermen for a franchise, and Sprague equipment was specified. Whitney's action seems to have broken the dam. By the end of the following year, 200 streetcar systems were either in operation or under construction in the United States, more than half actually equipped by Sprague, and more than 90 per cent based on his patents.

It was even a transatlantic triumph. Sprague lines were soon under way in Germany and Italy. On an 1889 Florence-Fiésole line, opening-day enthusiasm was dampened when a speeding car jumped a curve, killing several people and "wounding" others. This

One of the carbarns on the Richmond system. Changes and improvements in the trolley-pole mount came fast in the early years; and the car in front uses a pole of the third design in service. This dates the picture at about 1889 or 1890.

appears to have been a case of motorman error, and on that line control circuits were immediately modified so that the conductor could take over from the rear whenever he felt it advisable. This peculiar circuitry symbolized the relationship in a streetcar crew that has almost always been true: the conductor is captain of the ship.

No sooner did Sprague's company plunge into the fast-spreading development after Richmond than it found itself in slam-bang competition with a vigorous new rival. At one point in the Richmond days Sprague had been offered a chance to buy Van Depoele's company, then very shaky. "But, partly because of confidence in my own work and lack of appreciation of Van Depoele's—to say nothing of our own resources being taxed to the limit—it was not considered." This may have been a mistake. Van Depoele had slight patent primacy on the trolley, and

he was shortly to discover that carbon brushes were vastly better than those of metal, a discovery that greatly improved motors and dynamos everywhere. At any rate his firm was bought by the Thompson-Houston Company, of Lynn, Massachusetts. This was a lively concern that promptly jumped into the electric-railway business, speedily became Sprague's keenest rival, and even pried away a part of Whitney's Boston electrification. There were so many contracts to be had after Richmond, however, that the competition didn't hurt.

Late in 1889, after only about a year and a half of all-out activity, the Sprague Electric Railway & Motor Company was absorbed by the Edison General Electric Company. It is difficult to tell how Sprague felt about this loss of control, but apparently it wasn't initially displeasing. Johnson and later Edison General Electric had after all advanced Sprague

This photo puzzles sharp-eyed trolley experts. It is supposed to show Sprague's simultaneous-start demonstration in 1888.

But some cars above have trolley-pole bases not used until the following year. Probably the stunt was restaged in 1889.

Easing downgrade with the motorman tightening up on the hand brake, an early Richmond open car displays casually furled side curtains. Among street-railway men, word spread quickly that electrics were cheaper to run than horsecars.

a good deal of money, and he had had a close and amiable relationship with the larger company, which had built much of his equipment. But shortly after the consolidation, the weather changed drastically. Not all of Sprague's associates were kept on by the new firm. Orders were issued to eliminate the word *Sprague* from not only all new installations but also from the 113 existing ones and substitute "Edison-GE." Finally, as a last straw, a plan was announced for the abandonment of trolleys in new city systems in favor of a pet Edison idea of feeding extremely low voltages via the running rails. This wasn't a practical notion, as Leo Daft had spent years discovering; and Sprague himself called it "a retrograde attitude that for a time adversely affected the company's business."

Embittered, Sprague quit Edison-GE. Some of his associates who hadn't been hired after the merger went to Westinghouse, and he noted that that company "soon entered the railway field, but with ex-

cellent engineering." His bitterness toward the Edison-GE Company didn't last long; it was soon reorganized by J. P. Morgan (omitting the name Edison) and it soon absorbed Thompson-Houston, too. But Sprague seems to have retained a gentle asperity toward Edison for years. As late as 1928 he was mildly chiding *The New York Times* for overstating the importance of the Menlo Park railroad.

It would be a mistake to think of Frank Sprague as a professional holder of grudges; he was too busy, and too gifted, to indulge in more than a passing tartness. After Richmond he went on to a dazzling succession of achievements. In 1892 he helped design an eye-popping 1,000-horsepower electric locomotive, then by far the world's biggest. The following year he began building high-speed electric elevators with revolutionary control systems. They were better than anything seen before, and are now held to have been an important factor in encouraging the widespread construction of skyscrapers in the United States.

In 1895 he began work on what was perhaps his most important invention, something called "multiple-unit control." This is a basic and ingenious method of precisely controlling a number of electric motors from a single location. It has made possible the efficient functioning of subway and elevated trains, as well as many electrified railroads. He sold these patents to General Electric and then promptly invented a wholly different way of governing many cars and sold *those* patents to Westinghouse.

In 1902 he was a consultant on the electrification of the New York Central. The same year he also invented the famous "dead man's button" on the controller, which automatically shuts off power and applies brakes if a motorman should doze off or faint. On innumerable occasions since, this device has saved whole trainloads of passengers from disaster. During the First World War he helped design depth charges and armor-piercing shells. In 1928 he unveiled a strange and potentially valuable system for running two separate elevators in the same shaft. On his seventy-fifth birthday he was tendered an impres-

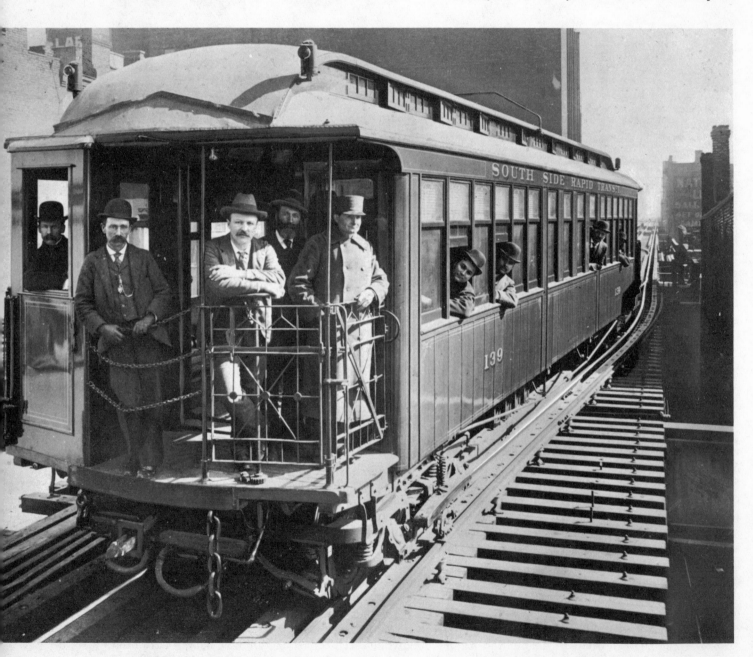

The world's first multiple-unit train control, the technical invention that made modern subways possible, was introduced on Chicago's South Side Elevated in late 1897. Sprague, its inventor, is the derbied man in the motorman's cab at left.

In shirtsleeves and sailor straw, Sprague poses at the master controller handle of the first workable multiple-unit car. It was July 16, 1897, and the place was an experimental track of General Electric's, near Schenectady, N.Y. The weed-grown track ran along one bank of the Erie Canal. In some respects this invention outshone even the trolley car.

sive celebration dinner by some of the country's most distinguished engineers and was greatly embarrassed by their fulsome tributes on a network radio broadcast. In 1934, laden with medals, degrees, and honors and still working hard on several unfinished inventions, he died.

It was a long, long way from that night in Richmond when a harried young man had dispatched Ensign Greene to fetch the four-legged instruments —and had founded a multibillion dollar institution that would be entwined in American life for decades to come.

Frank Sprague in 1932, still busy with new inventions at 75.

7. THE TROLLEY TRIUMPHANT

What on earth we're coming to,
Does anybody know?
For everything has changed so much
Since twenty years ago.

—From a speech of a trolley
company president in 1904

However halting and uncertain electric cars were at birth, there has rarely been a lustier child. In a handful of years horsecars were routed, cable cars were shoved onto a steep downslope, and the triumphant trolleys were carrying six times as many passengers as all the steam railroads in the country. In Brooklyn, so many car lines wound through the streets that the local baseball team was named the Trolley Dodgers, soon shortened to Dodgers.

Once a trolley even threatened to become a major factor in national politics: it came within a whisker of killing the President of the United States. It thereby nearly promoted the Secretary of State— John Hay—to chief executive, for the President was then himself a promoted Vice President. The man was Theodore Roosevelt, the place a dusty road outside Pittsfield, Massachusetts, the time September 3, 1902, almost a year after McKinley's assassination. The President and Governor Crane of Massachusetts were tooling along in an elegant landau drawn by four prancing white horses. Facing them was George B. Cortelyou, later the Secretary of Commerce and Labor, and up on the box were the driver and Secret Service man William Craig. Five outriders under the direction of Pittsfield Police Chief Nicholson were trotting along as escort, too far away, to their subsequent mortification, to figure at all in the accident. A carriage-load of newspapermen, to *their* embarrassment, had gone on ahead to the destination, a country club.

An open trolley, going in the same direction, overtook the presidential carriage. Aboard were a number of Pittsfield notables including two top officers of the streetcar company; it was later rumored and denied that they had ordered the motorman to hurry so that they could get to the country club in time to welcome the President. The trolley was in the center of the road and the landau on the right; well ahead of both vehicles was a place where the car tracks swung from the center of the road to the right side. Concentrating on his prancing team and unaware that a trolley was passing, the driver veered over the tracks. The landau was hit hard on its rear left wheel; the impact tipped it and shoved it aside, pitching its occupants into the air.

The President of the United States tumbled in the dirt, receiving a bruise on his cheek, a banged knee, a cut lip, and a severe shaking-up. His glasses were knocked flying, his silk hat was frazzled, his frock coat was torn at one elbow. According to *The New York Times* he told the horrorstruck motorman, "I think this is the most damnable outrage I ever heard of." Governor Crane and Secretary Cortelyou received only minor injuries, but the landau driver was seriously hurt and Secret Service man Craig—who had stood up at the instant of impact to protect the President—was thrown under the trolley and killed. The motorman, Euclid Madden, was fined 500 dollars and sent to jail for six months. Many streetcar men, believing that the accident was not solely his fault, were convinced that Madden was the victim of incredibly bad luck and of newspaper hue and cry.

By the turn of the century there were more than 15,000 miles of electrified track in the United States, more than 30,000 trolleys, and more than 2 billion dollars invested in traction companies. It was almost an explosive growth, so fast that it astounded even such professional optimists as trolley promoters.

Many reasons accounted for the sudden expansion. Horse and cable cars had developed operating details that could be borrowed complete—coin boxes, transfers, standard schedules, and fare registers. More important, they had established public attitudes and habits. "Taking the cars" was not a strange idea. The fact that trolleys had hesitated all through the

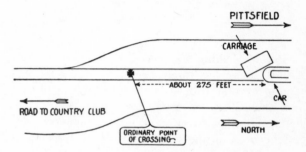

Smashed as it swung in front of a passing trolley, President Roosevelt's landau (left) looked like this afterwards. Though hit on the far side, its righthand wheels were broken when it was shoved sideways. The diagram below was prepared by the Street Railway Journal, *which had difficulty in accepting a presidential theory that it was all the motorman's fault.*

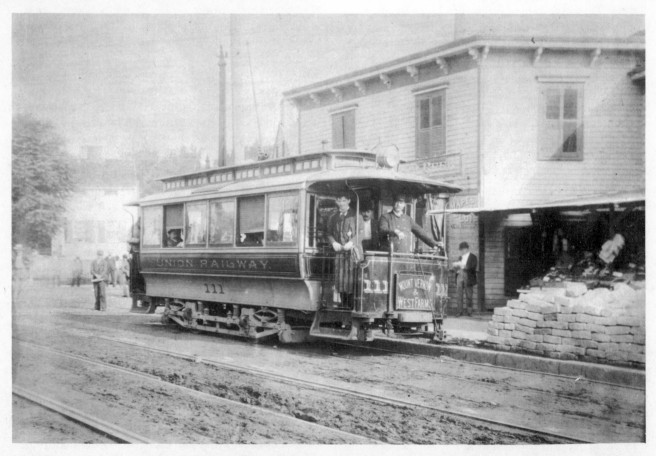

Capable cars like this one (built in 1895) made their way up from the Bronx to Westchester County, N.Y. The Union *Railway later became part of the Third Avenue System. The motorman in this 1905 photograph evidently liked his job.*

eighties on the brink of becoming technically practical may actually have sped their later growth; in their first decade most of the electro-mechanical equipment that was to see them through the great years was introduced. By the turn of the century there were durable motors, air brakes, good controllers, and alternating-current distribution systems.

The times, too, were wonderfully propitious. In the last three decades of the nineteenth century the country had nearly doubled its population. Older cities seemed to be bursting their seams, and new ones were springing up. By 1900 the national rate of population growth was steadily accelerating, and had moved past 1,330,000 new citizens each year. A glittering image of a prosperous, multiplying society was spreading among hard-headed businessmen everywhere. An electric streetcar system was a perfect symbol of municipal worth, a conspicuous demonstration of how much the town had grown and how exciting were its prospects. Unlike a steam railroad, which might be vital to a city but was often alien to it, governed by remote and unknowable men, a trolley line was *local*.

The trolley car was the latest thing, scientific and advanced. It was fast, able to achieve fully three times the old horsecar speeds. Plainly it was going to open up vast new residential areas, with intoxicating possibilities for real-estate profits. It wasn't unreasonably expensive to build, it was actually cheaper to operate than a horse or cable road, and it was a cinch to finance: its bonds were immediately snapped up by shrewd local capitalists with a faith in the city's future.

For the next few decades Americans everywhere were in love with their trolleys, in a warm surge of national affection that was later to be withdrawn and bestowed upon the automobile. And in return, trolleys spread and grew into a fine flowering. Soon they changed the homes, habits, and even courtship patterns of United States citizens.

Amusement parks, built by traction companies as "traffic generators," soon sprang up outside nearly every good-sized city in the land. In the cool of a summer Saturday evening, the ride out set the keynote, as these verses from the *Street Railway Journal* suggest:

> Oh, what delight
> On a soft June night
>   To ride in an open car!
> You can stand the expense—
> It's only five cents—
>   No matter how poor you are.

> In the three rear pews
> You may smoke if you choose;
>   'Tis the rule of the open car.
> But you'll hear, I'm afraid,
> Some fussy old maid
>   Say "Oh, that horrid seegar!"

The earliest parks were modest affairs—a little

Brill Dedenda Alarm Gong

THE Dedenda responds to each pressure on the pedal by a clear, penetrating note. There can be no chattering of the clapper as it is so constructed that it must rebound from the gong. Gongs come in 8, 12 and 14-in. sizes. Give thickness of crown piece.

A phantom drawing reveals where the clanging noise came from.

Big 14-bench open cars carried summertime throngs to Hampton Beach from Haverhill, Mass. It was a one-day vacation.

land bought for a carbarn or substation, with a few acres set aside as a picnic grove or ball park. Soon, though, they grew greatly and separated into two general categories—the park specializing in rural pleasures, and the ones where the calliopes called the tune.

An example of the former was Overlook Park, north of Dayton, Ohio, where the traction company had bought an 80-acre farm as a site for a generating station and carbarn. More or less as a by-product, part of the space was devoted to a picnic ground and dance hall:

A wide verandah extends around the dance hall, which is heated in winter by a pipe from the power station. There is an elevated platform for an orchestra, and a Cecilian automatic piano. The night foreman at the carbarn does double duty on evenings when there are dances. He plays selections on the automatic piano, and in the intermissions he goes back to the car house to look after his work. The grounds are free to all who come in the company's cars. Numerous swings have been provided, and a number of rowboats have been placed in

Vaudeville promised on the dashboard sign was at Highland Lake, Conn., on the Torrington & Winchester Street Railway.

the river, which is exceptionally fine for boating and fishing.

These pastoral facilities were overshadowed by such big and exciting places, many of them originally founded by trolley companies, as Elitch's Gardens at Denver, Savin Rock at New Haven, Jantzen Beach at Portland, Oregon, Coney Island Park at Cincinnati, Glendale Park at Nashville, and Revere Beach and Norumbega Park at Boston. Here immense crowds jammed the open cars—on a summer Saturday at Norumbega, fully 15,000 people would click through the turnstiles (five cents if you came by trolley, ten cents otherwise). At many parks the company saw to it that there was no other way to get in except by trolley. Here could be found entertainment to suit every imaginable taste: rowboats and canoes; bathing and fishing; bowling and baseball; Crackerjack and steak dinners; band concerts and "elite vaudeville entertainments." There were roller coasters of alarming velocity, tunnels of love of certified darkness, and giant swings, carrousels, and Ferris wheels

At Alameda Park, not far from Butler, Pa., the pavilion was up on the hillside above the trolley station and track loop.

Streaming away from two Jersey Central Traction Company open cars, a horde of pleasure seekers head for the beach at Highlands, N.J., *on a Saturday afternoon. With hats like the one on the woman at right, the perils of freckling were slight.*

providing all degrees of vertigo. There were casinos, sheltered from summer showers, where you could see melodramas, drink beer, play penny-arcade games, demonstrate your strength with a mallet, or hire private rooms for fraternal banquets. There were public fountains of sulphur water, to be drunk with a dash of salt, to tone up your health. Menageries were carefully stocked to appeal to youngsters, specializing in lions guaranteed to roar and in wonderfully comical monkeys.

Often the favorite family rendezvous was the bandstand ringed by tree-shaded seats. At Philadelphia's Willow Grove Park the greatest attractions by far were Sousa's Band and the celebrated "Electric Fountain"—particularly pleasing after dark because of the romantic stimulus of red and blue lights on the spraying waters. In many parks a breathtaking display of skyrockets and aerial bombs signalized closing time on Saturday night. But trolley starters always found that it took fully an additional hour to round up the last few carloads of couples for the trip back to the city, and it was frequently necessary to run a number of "last cars" to ship the stragglers home.

The powerful leverage of romance was also employed to drum up business. Wonderland Park at Revere Beach energetically publicized a song that suggested that a trolley ride was almost an avenue to a girl's heart:

Wonderland, Wonderland, that's the place to be!
Each night when I call on my sweetie, she says to me:
"Let's take a trolley ride to the oceanside
Where the shining lights are grand."

Strung across the dash of each car on the line, the notice of a dance tonight was sufficient to energize many an uncommitted young swain. The motorman of this Clarksburg, W.Va., car is holding the controller handle, his badge of office.

At Coronado Beach, near San Diego, an ancient double-decked open car glides past the gaily striped canvas of Tent City.

If you want to make good as a true lover should,
Just take her to Wonderland!

In their heyday, street-railway parks had little of the faintly raffish and tawdry flavor that amusement parks later came to have. They were generally respectable, middle-class places. Rowdy customers were energetically suppressed: one Brooklyn company regularly hired seventy-five special policemen each summer to ride the cars to the beaches and act as "ruffian bouncers." The parks were accepted by all but the most fastidious. In 1904 a new attraction at Savin Rock, Connecticut, was a hardwood slide called "Chilcoot Pass, or Bump the Bumps." Of this the *Street Railway Journal* reported happily: "It has attracted many thousands in the seasons just past, and was by all odds the hit of the summer. Over its surface slid many thousands of visitors, Governor Benjamin Odell of the Empire State, together with a distinguished party of United States Supreme Court judges and others of like prominence, being notable patrons of the game." It isn't recorded whether this buffing by the Supreme Court added special luster, but Chilcoot Passes turned up all over the map the following season.

The same bustling vitality that built the electric parks was displayed in their promotion. Once the United Traction Co., of Reading, Pennsylvania, staged an elaborately advertised Elks Carnival at Carsonia Park that proved almost too successful. By drawing 70,000 paying customers in a few days, it nearly swamped the carrying capacity of the line, and the thought of what a breakdown might have done gave the management the shivers. This same company also pioneered with an ingenious gambit by which seats in the park theater were sold in blocks to merchants in town. The merchants would then advertise heavily that they were giving away tickets with each sizable purchase. This saved the company the expense of advertising the theater, but hordes of people would still come, arriving and departing by trolley.

As the potentialities of "created traffic" became evident, more and more trolley lines hired traffic managers and set up special departments to solicit business. Tips on ingenious come-ons frequently appeared in the trade press. They were directed mostly at small suburban and interurban lines that were presumed lacking in the enterprise of larger companies.

These ladies bustling from their open car are about to have a treat: a visit to the birthplace of John Greenleaf Whittier.

This special attraction could be found on the Massachusetts Northeastern Railway, between Haverhill and Merrimac.

Some typical suggestions:

1. Organize a baseball league with teams in communities along the trolley line. If necessary, supply players with free transportation, but avoid paying for uniforms or otherwise supporting the teams. "Greatly increased traffic will be created by local pride in home teams."

2. Make certain that passenger solicitors regularly look into the possibility of special excursions for Masons, Knights of Pythias, Odd Fellows, and the like.

3. Encourage the planning of county and other fairs. Do not overestimate the size of community necessary. "Even villages of only 1,000 pop. will often support a street fair if someone is enterprising enough to start the game."

4. Do not neglect the possibilities of encouraging special trolley excursions—office or factory picnics, trolley parties, dances, family reunions, veterans'

affairs, theater parties, skating parties and winter carnivals, sporting-event excursions, and personally conducted tours of interesting sites.

An active, even cockeyed, imagination often paid off in soliciting passenger traffic. Once the Pacific Electric Railway Company sweet-talked several National Guard companies into staging a sham battle as a trolley promotion:

A site was selected near the ocean that could be easily reached by two of the local Long Beach lines, and the land leased for the event. The troops were given their transportation, and the company also paid for the ammunition used and for other expenses. The sham battle was widely advertised in the local papers and by placards and handbills.

The result was that, on a spot where probably no more than thirty people had ever congregated before, there assembled a crowd of 10,000 people to witness the maneuvers. As each passenger paid 50 cents for the round trip it can be easily realized that the event was a money-maker for the company, the expenses being comparatively small. It was on this occasion that one car was observed carrying 160 people inside and 43 on the roof.

From the earliest days on, open cars were the summertime favorites of the trolley-riding public. In many communities the open-car trolley party had a vogue—a car chartered for an afternoon or evening jaunt, with group singing on the way home. Sometimes for big trolley parties there would be two or three cars, festooned with garlands of light bulbs and perhaps a hired band tootling away in the head car.

In sweltering weather traction companies would notice evening traffic increases on open-car routes, reflecting the numbers of people who rode the cars at random in the evening, just to cool off. In a day without movies, air conditioning, or electronic amusements, riding nowhere in particular on a hot evening

Whether for cooking lectures, Chautauqua, or revivals, most traction companies were delighted to charter special cars.

What could be more fun, on a summer's night in Milwaukee, than to charter "Marguerite" for a trolley party? The many- *hued bulbs made a bright splash in the darkness; the movable chairs were perfect for impromptu two-part harmonies.*

was a happy custom. Up front the motorman pulled down the green curtain that shielded his window from reflections. If a thunderstorm blew up, the conductor unfurled the flapping canvas side curtains and, when a passenger reached his stop, he briefly raised the section near his bench while those within crowded together to avoid a splashing.

But though the riding public loved open cars, the companies didn't. It was a considerable expense, for one thing, to buy and maintain extra rolling stock that could be used only a few months of the year. Some lines experimented with purchasing open-car bodies alone and mounting them each spring on trucks taken from the regular cars, but this turned out to be costly and cumbersome. Others elected to use special cars called "convertibles" or "semiconvertibles"—closed cars with center aisles and vestibule entrances, but with sides or windows that were either removable or capable of being slid up out of the way. Though breezier in summer than regular closed cars, convertibles were rarely as popular as the true opens. On lines where the two kinds were run intermixed, people with leisure would wait at the stop, disdainfully passing up the convertibles and waiting until a real open car came along.

From the company standpoint, open cars had the additional drawback of a slightly higher accident rate, with accompanying damage suits. People tended to board or leave open cars in motion; and while it was no trick to swing onto or down from a car that had slowed to 7 or 8 miles an hour, a missed handhold or slippery footing could land a man flat on his back. Street-railway men repeatedly commented in their trade papers about the curious pattern to boarding accidents. Men almost invariably got off a moving car facing forward, the natural and least dangerous way to do it; but women frequently attempted it facing backward, a practice that, when a car was moving faster than a walk, tended to send them cartwheeling head over teakettle. The consensus in the correspondence columns of the *Street Railway Journal* was that a substantial percentage of lady passengers could be depended on to have no sense whatever.

Yet there was only one time when the presence of pretty girls aboard a trolley wasn't welcomed by all. This was during the months in 1909 when the

The occasion that warranted so much bunting was a Shriners' outing at Hampton Beach, N.H., in 1901. It was only a dozen years after trolleys had first become practical, but large, reliable cars like these were a commonplace everywhere.

yellow press was full of daring revelations about the White Slave Trade. Tabloid headlines screamed of how innocent girls were captured for a Life of Degradation: they would be demurely riding a trolley when a white slaver would stab them with a poisoned needle, rendering them so dazed and pliable that they could then be hustled from the car. These stories won such credence that whenever a woman had an ordinary fainting spell on a car, all nearby males hastily edged as far away as possible. With the publication of calm statements from medical men that such poisoned needles didn't exist, and with the passage by Congress of the Mann Act in 1910, the anxieties were gradually put aside.

Another company prejudice against open cars arose from the nagging suspicion that plenty of nickels that should have been collected never were. On the big fifteen-bench open cars, with seats for seventy-five people, passengers swarmed aboard all along the side, and even the most capable conductor, swinging along the running boards, had a difficult job keeping track of who'd paid and who hadn't. Further discontent, from the company viewpoint, arose from the increased difficulty in obtaining accurate "spotting" by the plainclothes inspectors that most lines used to check up on the conductor's honesty. With a closed car a spotter could regularly

The vehicle that this lady is boarding with a careful, two-handed technique was known as a Narragansett-type open car.

Hurrying to a car for a return from the beach. Often it needed fancy footwork to establish who was going to sit by whom.

Railway post offices, with cancellation stamps marked "R.P.O.," were widely used, often making a circuit within a city.

compare the number of passengers entering a vestibule with the number of fares shortly rung up on the register. But on an open car with its spread-out loading area, a moderate amount of conductor larceny was extremely difficult to detect.

In addition to open cars, a great variety of special-purpose trolleys began to appear around the turn of the century. For use in operations and maintenance, there were sand cars, sweepers, snowplows, "big hooks" (crane cars, for unloading rail or tidying up after wrecks) and line cars. The latter, which looked like scaling platforms from a Roman siege, typically had extendable wooden platforms to permit linemen to work on the "overhead" and were sometimes specially rigged to pay out electrically connected wire for fast repairs. There were paymaster cars to travel to each carbarn on payday, and quick-lunch cars to serve up frankfurters and coffee to company employees—an anticipation of the final sad lot of many a regular trolley. There were bulgy-tanked sprinkler trolleys to wet down dusty streets, a service required

Sprinkler cars laden with great water tanks came out during dry spells to lay the dust on unpaved streets and to flush off the paved ones. Like this car, many had pivoted side pipes that swung out to spray their water over a wide swath.

under the franchise in some municipalities. Special postal trolleys, painted red, white, and blue and often provided with letter slots into which passers-by could insert rush communications, ran for years in large cities. In Virginia a trolley delivered cakes of ice to homes that displayed a card in a front window. In Montreal, Syracuse, and Chicago, trolley paddy-wagons, somberly barred and locked, shuttled felons from courthouse to jail.

In some cities it was the practice for the company to build cars in its own shops, though the trucks, control and brake systems, and similar parts were usually purchased from specialized makers. When brand-new cars of improved design were ready, it was exciting local news. The company would announce in the newspapers that at least one of the cars would be sent on each route all over town. People would line the streets for their first glimpse of the fine new trolleys.

Of all the curious kinds of trolleys that have been built, the private parlor cars were among the most exotic. Nominally intended for use by company offi-

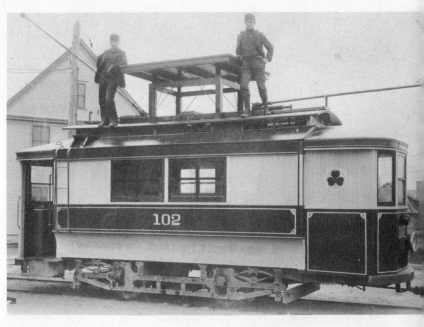

Though widely used, tower cars had one drawback compared to tower wagons: they couldn't pull aside to let cars go by.

Some companies built trolley-car bodies in their own shops, a task that demanded painstaking craftsmanship. The double- *truck car taking shape above was built about 1905 in the shops of the Colorado Springs & Interurban Railway.*

This private car was the pride and joy of the traction-company officers in Manchester, N.H. Its capacious observation platforms and lavish iron scrollwork were greatly admired.

cials on inspection trips, parlor trolleys appeared quite widely in the nineties. At first they seem to have been a conscious imitation of the elegant private cars in which railroad barons swanked about in clouds of Corona-Corona smoke. (Streetcar men always preferred to think of themselves as railroaders—a kingly occupation—and occasionally displayed a pushy eagerness to be admitted to the fraternity.)

Parlor-car trolleys were generally luxurious, with gleaming brass fittings, richly curtained windows, and wall-to-wall carpeting. Interiors ran to decorated ceilings, polished mahogany paneling, and perhaps colored glass in the clerestory. The directors of the Connecticut traction company could avail themselves in their car of a lavatory that was shielded from common gaze by stained-glass windows of almost paralyzing elegance. In Manchester, New Hampshire, the directors' car had enough fancy scrolled ironwork for a New Orleans building front; in Denver a parlor car had a "tasteful ceiling of Paris green, with dark green border ornamented in gold." This one also had sixteen rattan easy chairs, eight glittering spittoons, and mother-of-pearl call buttons with which a faint director could summon refreshment to his easy chair. In St. Louis the private car *Mabel* not only had special lockers for china, glassware, and linen, but also an icebox, sink, built-in desk, rich portières, opalescent glass, and an overstuffed loveseat.

Even though originally built to enhance the self-esteem of officials—it was after all a day when the conspicuous display of prosperity had good sanction—these de luxe trolleys soon found additional service on charter trips. Many a citizen would willingly plank down twenty or thirty dollars on spare-no-expense occasions such as weddings or anniversaries so that he could glide elegantly through the streets in publicly displayed privacy. Fraternal affairs, bachelor dinners, and special sightseeing tours for visiting dignitaries were other parlor-car occasions. Often, too, they were chartered for funerals.

Trolleys served as hearses in many cities. In Baltimore a special hearse car, felicitously named *Dolores,* was many times booked up to her full capacity of two or three funerals a day. Undertakers who were unable to sign up *Dolores* for an interment had to fall back on *Lord Baltimore,* a handsome, coal-black parlor car, but one lacking the special features that made *Dolores* so much in demand. These included a special casket compartment up front with a large glass door that allowed the coffin to be viewed from the street; a nickel-plated rail against which flowers could be banked; eight black leather seats in the casket compartment for first-degree mourners, and twenty-four seats in the rear for lesser grievers. The charge for all these somber but choice conveniences was moderate, twenty to twenty-six dollars, a fee that included the services of a neatly dressed motorman and conductor.

One vital piece of equipment on every trolley line

From company directors to chickens. The haughty private car pictured at the top of this page later sank to serving as a henhouse. The tale has a happy ending: the Seashore group of trolley fans has rescued it for restoration to past glory.

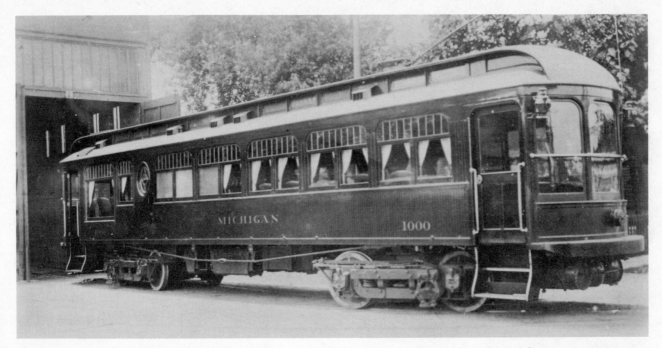

One luxurious touch in this Michigan Railway private car was the expanse of glass at the end for sightseeing in comfort.

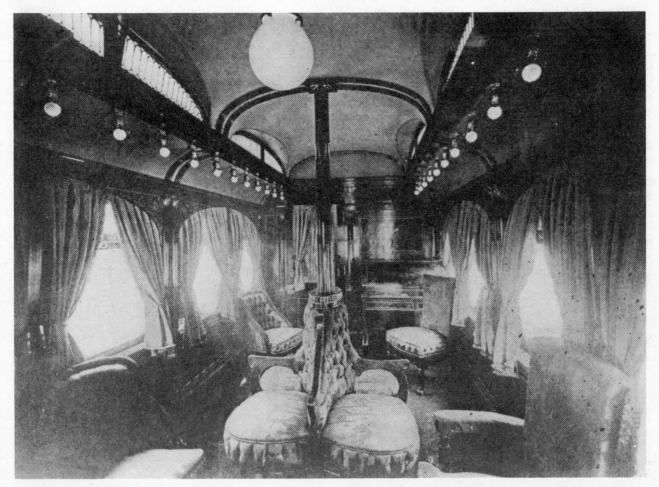

Interior of the private parlor car "Mabel," photographed in 1904. The leaded windows up high were of opalescent glass.

A trolley funeral in progress at Everett, Wash. In some respects a streetcar made a highly satisfactory hearse, because the family and friends could stay together on the trip.

was the little black book of rules that each employee was instructed to carry with him at all times. Read today, the early rulebooks suggest that the life of a motorman or conductor was colorful, dangerous, and fraught with complications. The following are from the rulebook of the Brooklyn Rapid Transit Company, shortly after 1900:

Employees are prohibited from entering saloons when in uniform, and from frequenting such places. Preference in employment and advancement will be given total abstainers.

Lying down or lounging in cars is prohibited. Conductors and motormen will never sit down while their car is in motion.

While engaged in operating a car, whistling, talking, or shouting to teamsters is forbidden, unless necessary to avoid an accident.

Should car become electrically charged, pole should immediately be pulled down.

The funeral car "Oregon" ran on the Providence and Danielson Street Railway in Rhode Island and Connecticut. Ceme- *teries were valuable on a trolley route not simply for funeral traffic but because people would ride out on weekends.*

Open at the top and closed below, this early double-decker in Tampa used two stairways in an effort to get fast loading.

Double poles and wires were used in Cincinnati because of the fear of electrolytic corrosion of pipes buried underground.

A Wilkes-Barre car in 1890. Exterior advertising signs, other than for the company, were never as popular here as abroad.

A battlefield tour by trolley was once popular among visitors to Gettysburg. The signs on the side announced stops at the   *Devil's Den, the Wheat Field, and the National Cemetery. The white-coated man alongside served as the car's porter.*

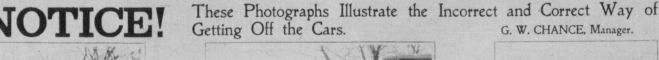

NOTICE! These Photographs Illustrate the Incorrect and Correct Way of Getting Off the Cars. G. W. CHANCE, Manager.

INCORRECT--Very Dangerous!
GETTING OFF IN OPPOSITE DIRECTION CAR TRAVELS.

THE RESULT!
Wait Until the Car Stops!!

CORRECT WAY to Get Off!
FACE ABOUT HALF WAY TOWARD FRONT OF CAR AND SIDE.

Many companies adopted a basic rulebook devised by the American Street Railway Association in 1903 and modified to suit local needs. These rules reflected the experience and the trouble spots of scores of companies. For example, ASRA Rule 3 (conductors and motormen must be clean and neat) and Rule 4 (they must treat passengers with politeness and must not make threatening gestures nor use loud, uncivil, indecent, or profane language, even under the greatest provocation) mirrored a continuing minor problem. This was the occasional employee who, beset by long hours, low wages, and the exasperations implicit in dealing with the public, lapsed into a kind of disheveled and throbbing misanthropy. In a little paper-backed treatise titled "How to Become a Motorman," a motorman-author named Rodger Burns wrote:

Do not lose control of your temper! Many a man of whom I have personal knowledge has lost his position because of a quick temper. I remember a motorman who was always ill-tempered. The minute he stepped in the vestibule and got his hand on the controller handle, he was angry at everyone and everything; there was never anything right; the conductor was too slow, or the passengers were too slow, or too many people were riding. He had an idea that everyone wanted to ride with him, and that they brought all the old women, little children, and cripples on his car so he could not make his

time. He thought there was always a rig crossing ahead of him that had no business to, and that they never paid any attention to his gong. He was in a rage all the time, and I personally know of one accident that he was entirely to blame for, which could have been avoided if he had not lost his temper.

Do not forget your personal appearance. Nothing gives a motorman a better stand in the public eye than to be clean and neatly dressed. If there is anything that disgusts me in a fellow worker, it is to sit behind him in a car and gaze on a neck so dirty that you could raise a crop of potatoes on it without any fertilizer.

Many of the ASRA rules were evidently prompted by the growing national tendency to sue streetcar companies for real or fancied injury. By the early years of this century the trend had progressed to the extent that, after wages, power, and maintenance, the damages extracted by plaintiff's lawyers were one of the bigger operating costs. Many of the rules reflected sensitive areas:

"Do not remove trolley from wire at end of run at night until all passengers have alighted from car." Here the problem was that of the passengers tumbling litigiously out of the darkened vestibule. "Conductors and motormen must in a polite way endeavor to keep people from jumping on and off the cars while in motion." This was little more than a pious doctrine until cars were equipped with gates or doors that

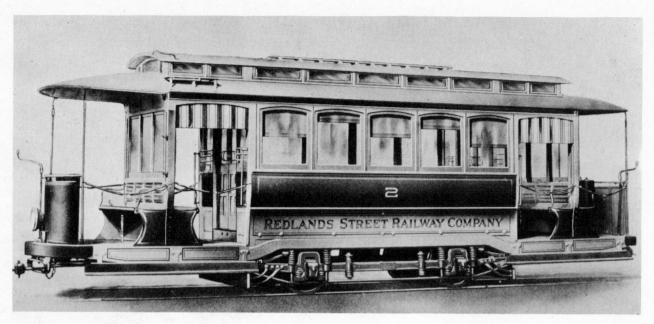

Developed in the west where the climate is mild, car bodies that combined open and closed features became nationally known as "California" cars. This early single-truck street car, built by Brill, proved a little small for combining.

Longer combination cars, divided at the middle, had a vogue in the east, particularly in New York City. After a time it grew evident that the operative factor was not a matter of varying tastes but of the weather; if it was mild and pleasant everybody wanted to sit outside, and if not they all crowded together inside. This picture was taken in 1898.

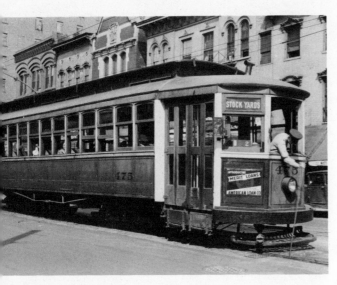

When a magnetic track switch didn't flip over properly, most motormen would swear, slam on the brakes, and then get out (or lean out, as above) to pry it over with a switch iron.

could physically restrain impatient riders. "Passengers must not be allowed to carry bulky or dangerous packages aboard cars . . . or any dogs except such small ones as can be carried in the lap." Some conductors developed delusions that a disproportionate number of men carrying bass viols, two-man saws, rolls of barbed wire, and kegs of fish fertilizer attempted to board their cars. When they succeeded, it always seemed to develop that fat women would lurch crunchingly against the bass viols, or that fragile, jury-appealing people would wound themselves on wire or saw. Or that a grandmother type would take one whiff of the fish barrel and swoon at a lawyer's feet, developing lower-back pain as she fell.

Ejection of unruly or nonpaying passengers proved to be a particularly sore point:

No passenger shall be forcibly ejected from a car for any cause whatsoever, unless the conduct of the passenger is dangerous and grossly offensive. The ejectment must be made by the conductor with the assistance of the motorman after the car has been brought to a stop, using only such force as is sufficient to expel the offending passenger with a reasonable regard to his personal safety.

No passenger will be ejected for mere intoxication, unless said passenger becomes dangerous or offensive; such passenger must then be ejected with great care, and must be guided until free from probable injury. Always get names of witnesses, and make a report of the same as in case of accident. No passenger shall be put off at a point where likely to be exposed to danger. Particular attention must be paid to this rule during inclement weather, late at night, or when a passenger is intoxicated.

Here plainly was real corporate anxiety. The hazards were twofold. Not only might an ejectee, hurtled into the hazardous night by an overzealous crew, end up in a state where he or his widow could win whopping damages, but worse, he might get taken up by the newspapers as an example of the heartlessness of the traction company. In a number of cities the relations between the newspapers and the streetcar lines were distinctly hostile. Newspapers tended to the view that the company had to be watched like a hawk and frequently required instruction in the most elementary aspects of providing public service. Many companies, on the other hand, felt that newspapermen were irresponsible gadflies, ignorant of the problems of railroading and interested solely in distortions and sensationalism. How far this mutual distrust developed is implied by ASRA Rule 57: "No employee shall, under any circumstances, give any information whatsoever concerning any accident of any kind to any person except to a properly authorized representative of the company." Mum, in short, was the official word.

Faked accidents with their false injury claims were a persistent problem. Three favorite kinds were stumbles on boarding, a pedestrian seemingly sent sprawling by the outward swing of a car on a curve, or a showy, windmilling fall from a platform or step. One professional injury claimant had considerable success for a time by bringing along his own banana

Sometimes an amiable conductor would do the honors with the switch iron. This heavy bar, along with a brake handle or reverse key, was also useful for overawing difficult drunks.

The first electric car in Omaha, Nebr. Its motorman had the dignified and proper mien that was suited to this honor.

peel as a plausible stage setting for his artistic tumbles. A few accident fakers were benefited in their trade by old, mis-set fractures or skeletal anomalies; these produced X rays of internal dishevelments so pronounced as to loosen up the most tight-fisted juries. The best weapon that company investigators had against professional victims was evidence of a series of damage awards in other cities, and much information to this end was circulated between companies and in the trade press.

On New York's Lower East Side some accidents developed into stylized rituals, like the mating of trumpeter swans. A trolley would be moving along congested and turbulent Delancey Street when a pushcart would somehow carom off its side or rear, dumping its contents on the street. Instantly loud caterwauls would arise and hundreds of people would gather to curse the rich and callous traction company. In court later so many witnesses for the plaintiff would appear, all voluble and eager to testify about the trolley's reckless speed, that company lawyers found it virtually impossible to win such suits. To cut losses, it became the practice to settle such claims by equally stylized ritual; a *reasonable* number of pushcart accidents a month, properly executed and with witnesses marshaled, would be routinely settled in

Trolleys rapidly grew so common in the first flush of success that they risked collision daily. Rochester, N.Y., in 1900.

The men who ran the trolley cars of Saginaw, Mich., in 1893. Most of them had learned their trade on horsecars.

advance for a flat fee of twenty-five dollars.

In recent years, motormen and conductors have sometimes been thought of as crochety men on the far slopes of middle age. This was untrue in the great years of the trolley, when car crews were often youngsters in their early twenties. Many a motorman would admit in confidence that he had three ages: his actual age; his "working-papers age," advanced a year or two; and his traction-company age, perhaps moved up still another year to pass a twenty-one-year-old hiring requirement. Only occasionally would a motorman be in his forties, and of him it might be rumored in the carbarns that he was working under an assumed name, after a fatal accident in another city. (This was not necessarily pure fancy: after a bad accident it was traditional for a motorman to leave for parts unknown. Some companies fell into the tradition and renumbered any car that had been involved in a severe accident.)

For all its rulebooks and harassments, a motorman's or a conductor's life in the heyday of the trolley could be a fine, satisfying career. As Rodger Burns observed in his handbook: "There are not many trades at which a man can work where manual labor is eliminated much more than that of a motorman. You can wear good clothes and be out in the open air, which is much more healthful than to be shut up in a dirty shop. You see the sunshine and the flowers, and are out among the people and have an idea what the world is doing."

Apart from the brass-buttoned blue uniform and hat—which the company usually made a motorman

Intercepted after riding on the Pittsburgh trolleys for nineteen straight hours, Jimmy Crawford, aged 7, said he wanted very much to be a motorman as soon as he grew up.

pay for—there were many intangible rewards to the job. There was the open-eyed fascination with which youngsters watched the manipulation of controller, brake, sanding lever, and gong. Virtually all small boys and some little girls could plainly see that a motorman's life was an enviable one. (These were the same kids, grown a few years older, who greased the rails on Halloween or who developed the knack of jerking the trolley off the wire.) There were the ceremonious conversations, as among equals, with the firemen and policemen who rode in the vestibule. On a regular run in a residential neighborhood there was the warming way in which riders came to greet a motorman by name and exchange judicious comment on the weather. Most important of all, there was the reward of friendly trust, evidenced by the way a hard-drinking carouser would snooze away on an owl run, confident that the trolley crew would wake him for his stop and, if needful, help him up his porch steps.

In all its forms—open car and closed, parlor car and hearse—the trolley prospered and worked its way deeply into American life. It was hard to imagine the land without it.

A town that didn't have at least one trolley line found it difficult to keep up its self-esteem. Brooding over the trolley-less situation of the village of Croghan, N.Y., a postcard photographer resolved to remedy it. He plunged into his darkroom and emerged with this locally popular but entirely bogus photograph. It did make people feel a little better.

8. THE EMPIRE
OF THE INTERURBANS

Today the old roadbed, like an Indian mound, winds down through the woodlands; the rails, wire, and ties are long ago sold; the embankments are crumbled and overgrown; and gone forever from the valley is the mellow whistle of the interurban.

—C. C. Duncan

An alert eye can occasionally detect small evidences today, in both countryside and city, of the great empire of the interurbans—the electric-railway network that sprang up about sixty years ago, flourished widely and a little wildly, and, barring a few atypical lines, has now completely vanished. Sometimes the clue is a characteristic form to a shabby roadside diner or hen house, proclaiming that it once rumbled proudly at 60 miles an hour. Sometimes the evidence is a gasoline station or garage that bears marks of an earlier incarnation as substation or carbarn. Most often the sign is a weedy or tree-grown right-of-way that, like a millrace or canal bank, shows only by the shape of the land that a wholly different way of life once existed there.

Your first ride on an interurban, years ago, was not soon forgotten. Usually the terminal was near the middle of the city, with the big car awaiting you in an off-street train shed. Baggage and mail would have been loaded when you climbed aboard, giving a heave on the grab handle to mount the high first step. The interior seemed a marvel of luxury to a youngster who had known only ordinary city trolleys: carpeted floors, upper window panels of stained glass, and seats finished in rich green plush or black leather of wonderful smoothness. Up front, dressed in clean overalls, the motorman checked his air gauge, snapped the reverse key forward, and performed arcane rites with breakers and switches. Standing by the back step with watch in hand, the blue-uniformed conductor called out *"Bo-a-rd!"* Slowly and heavily the big car crept out of the shed, clanging its compressed-air gong and ponderously joining the flow of rigs and wagons on Main Street.

Through the city the car seemed to move with infinitely more caution and dignity than an ordinary trolley. The motorman constantly turned his head left and right, alert lest something venture too close. With a deep, resonant tone, the air compressor began its *nok-nok-nok.* Sharp turns in the city were navigated at a slow pace, the conductor in back peering out to watch the swing of the overhang and signaling the motorman to proceed.

Then at the edge of town the car swung off the pavement onto its private right-of-way and the motorman reached back to hitch up his wooden stool, for the anxieties of city traffic were past. Steadily he notched up his controller until the handle was against its stop. The continuing acceleration of the car was astonishing; it went faster and faster until you were secretly afraid it might leave the rails. The poles at the trackside seemed to stream past like fence posts, and out the rear there was a tremendous swirl of dust and cinders.

Beneath the floor the motor gave a steady, rising hum as background to the click of rail joints and the hiss of the trolley on the wire. Everywhere you saw the details of true railroading: electric signal lights gleaming down the track, switchstands with brightly colored targets, a dispatcher in shirt sleeves and vest at a junction holding up train orders for the crew. The car sped through the countryside, into deep cuts and across marshland on wooden trestles. Whenever a whistle post flashed by, the motorman reached for the cord to sound a thrilling *Hoo, hoooo, hoo-wah* and the crossing bell would whip past startlingly, changing pitch as it faded behind.

As a wide-eyed youngster, perhaps the most exciting experience was the first time you boarded an interurban at night at a deserted rural stop. A grown-up relative would come to see you safely aboard. Waiting at the open-sided shed in the darkness, you'd

Rocking smoothly along the straight steel rails, interurban riders could feel superior to travelers on bumpy dirt roads. This stretch was between Pontiac and Birmingham, Mich.

learn that an "intending passenger" was supposed to show a light. In the distance there would sound the faint hum of electric motors, and in a moment the wire overhead would begin to sing. If no lantern was handy, the grownup with you would roll up a sheet of newspaper and touch a match to it. Down the track the interurban would come rushing at 60 miles an hour, its arc headlight shining with a blue-white brilliance. If by accident the newspaper wasn't lighted soon enough, the car would most likely overshoot, braking to a stop several hundred feet along the track with angry blasts of compressed air. Leaning out his window as he backed up, the motorman would bawl out: "Hey, mister, show that light before I get by you! Think I can stop this car on a dime?"

Trolley historians tend to dispute about the exact definition of an interurban. The difficulty lies in establishing boundaries between city trolleys—which sometimes ran in suburban or country areas at brisk speeds—and electrified railroads that, in all but motive power, resembled steam railroads. In general, true interurbans traveled streets only to the edge of

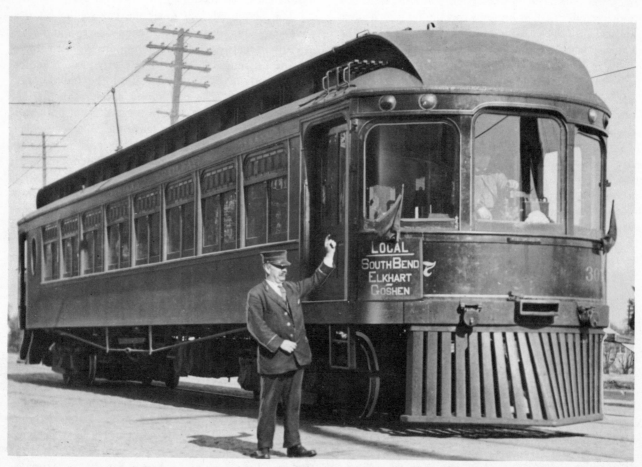

Interurban car in Indiana about 1911. The fearsome cowcatcher, known as a "pilot," was often made of wood rather than metal.

town and then rolled along a private right-of-way, sometimes adjoining highways but often cross-country. After the very first years, interurban cars were larger and heavier than their city cousins, and frequently bucketed along at 50 or 60 miles an hour. Unlike most steam lines, they usually concentrated more on passengers than on freight, and typically charged lower fares. The overhead trolley, however, was not always a distinguishing trait; interurbans also experimented with other current-collecting methods and with third rails.

The first interurbans turned up in the nineties, right after city trolleys became established. One of the earliest was a line that ran south from Sandusky, Ohio, to the towns of Milan and Norwalk, which began to carry passengers, mail, and freight on its 20 miles of track on December 1, 1893. Another Ohio line, the Akron, Bedford & Cleveland, began running between those cities in 1895. In Oregon a venturesome little line between Portland and Oregon City started service in February, 1893, and perhaps was the first interurban of them all.

At the beginning, interurbans did poorly. Both the Portland and Sandusky lines were in receivers' hands in less than a year. This was partly the times—the great growing weather for the big electric cars was a decade away—and partly it was mechanical unreliability. With continuous maintenance, an interurban car of the nineties had a useful life of five or six years. This was in contrast to the cars of eight or ten years later, which might be running yet if anyone wanted them. Describing the first Oregon cars, Randall V. Mills wrote:

When a motorman carelessly applied full power too suddenly, he would hear a bang and see a fine display of sparks spring from beneath the car, a cloud of acrid smoke burst up and drift away—and then silence. Then the car would be towed in, lifted from its trucks, and stripped of its motors; strong-armed shop crews, fighting long coils of stiff wire, would laboriously rewind the burned-out armature by hand, reassemble the motor, replace brushes, put the motor on the truck, put the trucks on the car, and wonder how long it would be before the act would require repeating.

About the turn of the century matters changed. As equipment grew more reliable, the belief spread

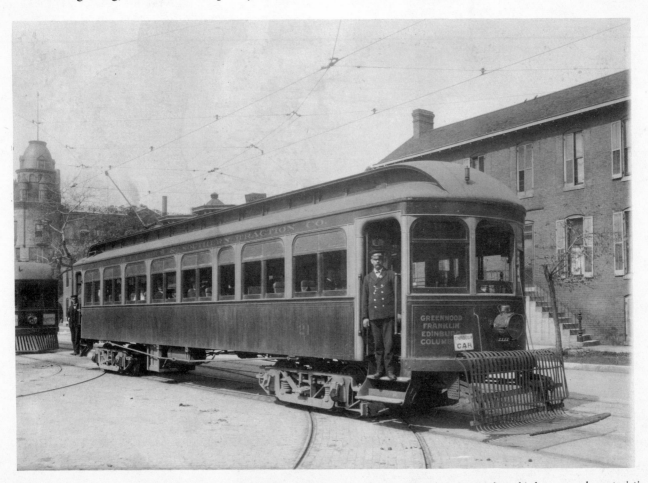

An early wooden interurban car leaving Indianapolis in 1905. The big headlight and upright whistle were characteristic.

*Running between Pittsburgh and But-
ler, Pa., this proud piece of varnish
used a trolley pole in town and a central pantograph in the country. The
crew members leaning so negligently
against the front of No. 111 in the 1913
photograph were conductor Dave Mc-
Donald and motorman Mother Frye.*

that interurbans were the coming thing in railroading. In just a few years a boom in interurban construction began. All over the country (though least in the mountain states and the deep South) interurbans pushed out like climbing vines to link cities and towns in a brand-new travel network. Just as in the middle of the nineteenth century every town pridefully strove to be on a railroad, now every town felt that it should have an electric link to its neighbors, even if it had to start building one itself. In the Middle West particularly, where interurbans had their lushest growth, many a line thrust out from small towns or even villages toward distant cities. Sometimes they went bankrupt before reaching their destinations, but even this didn't halt the spread of electric cars, because a wave of interurban consolidations soon came along. In many states large interurban systems were created by men who bought up sickly companies, building only the trackage necessary to link them together.

The growth wasn't purely spontaneous. To strum on the melodious chords of local pride and enhancement of property values, a specialized breed of interurban promoter appeared. He could cite the magnificent benefits to practically everyone that an electric line would bring: how farmers would be free to sell milk and produce wherever it would bring the most, instead of being exploited captives of just one nearby creamery or market; or how women would be liberated from the stupefying monotony of rural or hamlet life and could avail themselves of the improving opportunities of the city; how merchants could get one-day deliveries from distant warehouses, far quicker than by regular freight. There was also the whispered advantage that a man with the misfortune to live in a dry county could nip off to the city for a couple of bottles of rye with scarcely any effort at all. The interurban promoter, lineal descendant of the lightning-rod salesman of an earlier era, became so distinct and identifiable a phenomenon that he earned the title of a builder of "The Hot Air Line."

The strength of his spiel lay, of course, in its predominating admixture of truth. Interurbans *did* produce remarkable changes in many a rural area. As early as 1904 the *Street Railway Journal* was commenting, with unconscious patronage:

The sociological effect of an electric railway is also noticed along the Cazadero line. This country is settled largely by the pioneers of Oregon, who crossed the mountains and settled in this section some fifty years ago. Without transportation facilities and a 30-mile haul

An early Oregon car with its trailers, taken at Golf Junction.

A three-car train off for an outing at Olcott Beach, N.Y.

Rakish trolley poles, a lavish use of stained glass, and ornamental painting on the front and wooden sides added a touch of swank to this long Indianapolis-to-Terre Haute interurban.

necessary to market their goods, the advancement of these sturdy settlers has been slow. . . . It has taken the electric line to wake them up, and its benefit is evident on every hand. Fences have been improved, crops that were formerly fed to the hogs are now garnered and marketed, new barns and houses are being built, land is being cleared and new crops planted, the towns are growing and new ones being started, and a general enlightenment is seen everywhere.

Though many a line was projected and built in those giddy years without even a slim chance of succeeding, quite as many were laid down that, for a time, fulfilled every rosy expectation. In many places interurbans displayed such a lusty capacity to siphon off short-haul passengers and less-than-carload freight that some steam railroads were alarmed into countermeasures. In New York and New England, for example, railroads set about buying up control of the interurban lines that appeared to threaten them. (At high prices, too; the New Haven Railroad paid out so much that its later bankruptcy seems to have been accelerated.) In the Middle West the rivalry with steam created constant friction, concealed under the guise of safety considerations, at places where

interurban tracks wished to cross those of steam railroads. The interurbans, where they had to, built over- or underpasses, and cheerfully countered by offering such railroad comforts as diners and sleepers.

Promoters who talked confidentially about the eye-popping profits to be derived from real-estate enhancement could cite examples calculated to make a small-city capitalist almost itch with avarice. Perhaps the most glittering exhibit was Henry E. Huntingdon, whose Pacific Electric interurbans around Los Angeles were making money like a two-shift mint. This was a company whose unfettered instinct for promotion included plugging some sheet music called "The Pacific Electric Trolley Waltz." Huntingdon, a man with a highly developed instinct for gain, employed a land company and an interurban company in expert coordination. A basic gambit was to gain control of a great block of undeveloped and largely worthless land, and then have his interurbans lace through it. At first such an interurban branch might not be profitable, but the immediately skyrocketing land value would more than compensate for early losses. Pretty soon the territory would fill out and then both the interurban branch and the land

Ten big interurbans, chartered for a New York factory picnic.

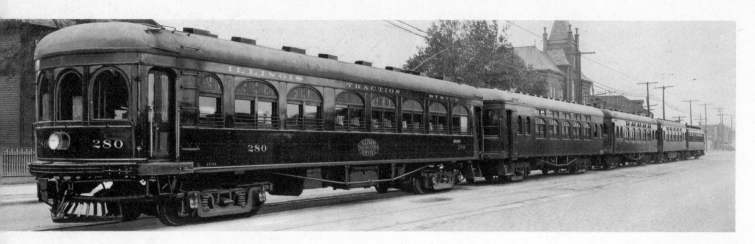

Sleeper runs, like this train from Peoria, Ill., shown arriving in Granite City, were occasionally tried out, though they never grew to much importance on interurban systems.

Steam railroads were often unwilling to allow their impudent rivals to build level track crossings. Under- or overpasses were the expensive solution where the conflict became sharp.

company would begin gathering in dollars in a fine torrent. A variant Huntingdon plan was to provide an interurban line for a consideration. If the principal landholders in an unserviced area decided that a line would be just what they needed, they usually had only to proffer Pacific Electric enough land, cash, or both to obtain the magic electric fertilization.

A millionaire in the grand tradition, Huntingdon built a private car in 1905 that was probably the most luxurious trolley in history. The *Alabama* was 63 feet long, weighed more than 51 tons, and could be loco-motive-drawn anywhere in the country like other private cars. When she reached home tracks, her motor gears were connected, the trolley raised, and four 200-horsepower motors fed the juice that could urge her smoothly along at speeds above 90 m.p.h. Late one night she once made a clear-tracks run from Los Angeles to Long Beach at an *average* 80 miles an hour. In addition to pure speed, the car offered such amenities as a pair of magnificent staterooms with double beds, a dining room that could provide a ceremonious dinner for ten guests, sufficient carved mahogany and silken drapes to shame lesser million-aires, and the companionable warmth of a wood-burning fireplace. Though Huntingdon sold his inter-urban line in 1910, he kept the *Alabama* for a few years longer. In the twenties she turned up on the

Henry E. Huntingdon, president of Pacific Electric Railway.

Huntingdon's private car, the "Alabama," was in 1905 the last word in electric-car elegance and high-speed performance.

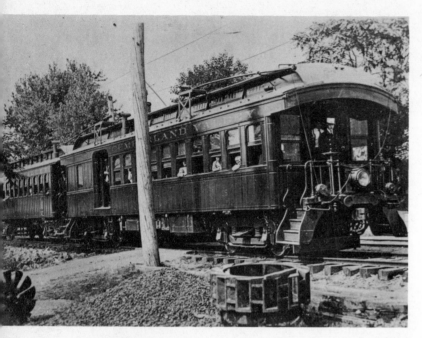

Four trolley poles, two on each side of the roof, were fitted to this 1909 car. It ran on the Cumberland Valley (Pa.) line.

Sacramento Northern, modified for service on de luxe passenger runs. One day in 1931 a percolator in her kitchen short-circuited, and soon the gaudy old car was reduced to smoking embers.

Vastly different were the cars in the years when interurbans were growing most rapidly. These were mainly wooden cars—steel ones came in around 1910—with roof ends rounded down in railroad fashion, and with a top speed on level rail of maybe 60 miles an hour, if the trolley voltage wasn't low. In a fine article in *Railroad Magazine,* C. C. Duncan wrote of the Illinois Valley Railway:

When I was a boy an interurban line was extended into our quiet town, and it brought us a new outlook on life. Where before we had moved about mainly by horse and carriage, we now rode forth grandly on plush seats to places 20, 30, and even 50 miles away. . . .

She was a typical wooden-bodied double ender of her day. The brass whistle stood stiffly where the trolley was held down by its hook, the body sat high on the trucks, heavy cowcatchers protected each end, and the commodious platforms were wide enough to carry a dozen

Followed by a city car, a Jersey Central interurban car rolls circumspectly along Broad Street in Red Bank, N.J.

The tallest structure on any interurban system was this steel trestle on the Fort Dodge, Des Moines & Southern, 3 miles north of Boone, Iowa. It soared 156 feet above the valley.

milk cans or chicken crates. She rumbled down to the north end of town, changed her trolleys, turned her seats, and rumbled back and departed. There were two compartments, the smoker and what was called· the "ladies' parlor." The former had rattan seats, plain floor, and cuspidors. It was a rough place, for the cigar-smoking, tobacco-chewing male. The Ladies' Parlor was much different, with plush seats, carpet on the floor, and bulkheads grained to simulate Circassian walnut.

Interior lights burned day and night, for by their brilliance or dimness the crew could judge the amount of power in the lines. The lights also gave instant warning of the trolley's jumping the wire. Our power was never too good, and the illumination always faded to a

Plagued by a hilly line, the Southern Cambria Railway in Pennsylvania had more than its share of wrecks. At the top, one of the derailments in Conemaugh; below, the crash at Brookdale.

dim glow on starting, or on a grade. If a travel-weary passenger sought diversion in reading, he was likely to find himself in long periods of electrical twilight. There was of course no ventilation other than open windows. To open one of these generally took considerable strength—the car could be loose and worn in every joint, but never the sash. In the winter a heating system consisting of a coal burner and hot water pipes went into action. It was marvelously efficient, for the car was always heated to the point of suffocation.

Our waiting room contained benches, a ticket window, an old-fashioned magneto telephone, and a bulletin book. People there talked knowingly of such places as Sinkerson's Cut, Shaffer's Crossing, Bureau, and Location. . . . Conductor-motorman Oscar Hanson stolidly piloted his car back and forth, letting it run itself unattended while he collected fares—in those traffic-less days a practice not as dangerous as it sounds now.

Most interurban lines had one or two severe accidents—resounding head-on collisions with the cars telescoped in splinters and the customers expiring by the dozen. Considering that the bulk of the mileage was single-tracked, with traffic flowing briskly in both directions and often governed only by primitive telephone-dispatching methods, it was a wonder there weren't more "cornfield meets." Nautical traditions of staying with the ship didn't always apply to motormen. If, wheeling along at high speed, a motorman suddenly spied the front of another car racing grimly toward him, it was held proper for him to "join the birds" once he applied emergency braking or reversed the motors. This was premised on the notion that he had done all there was to do, and that survival up front was unlikely. On downhill runaways, though, when brakes had failed, a motorman was normally expected to stay with his car.

Serious collisions had a distressing tendency to happen on holidays or festive occasions, when extras or specials, not in the timetable, were out on the line. In many a company's history there is record of a Fourth of July or Decoration Day or Thanksgiving crash when some crew forgot to phone in at a meeting point, and the extra and a regular came lethally together around a bend. On very few lines, nevertheless, were there accidents of such frequency and severity as to discourage the customers. One exception to this was the Southern Cambria Railway, a star-crossed line in hilly Pennsylvania terrain. It had such a continuing string of accidents that, in its declining years in the 1920's, only a small number of hardy passengers could be coaxed aboard. The unfortunate SCR had so many runaways that, in the town of Conemaugh alone, three houses and a school were on various occasions demolished by derailed cars. Its worst accident was in 1916 at Brookdale, where an excursion-car crash killed 28 and injured 80. But SCR's grim record was unusual.

The great preponderance of interurban accidents were less spectacular: crossing collisions, or the demise of livestock munching on the right-of-way, or comparatively innocuous derailments and split switches. A line in New York State provided its motormen with a stock of bright red envelopes, each with the word "WARNING" printed on the outside in ominous black letters. On spotting a tramp strolling along the tracks, the motorman was supposed to tootle vigorously and toss the envelope at the intruder's feet as the car sped by. Inside the envelope, interested and literate tramps could read the following message:

All persons are forbidden to use the tracks or any portion of this company's right-of-way for footways or thoroughfares. The practice is dangerous and unlawful.

Severe telescoping was typical in head-on collisions. This happened in 1915 on the Empire State Railways at Minetto, N.Y.

On Sept. 10, 1910, 33 people were killed at Kingsland, Ind., in one of the worst interurban collisions.

All persons so doing are trespassers and will be subject to prosecution. The company is not liable for injury or accidents.

As with city trolleys, boarding and alighting accidents were a continuing headache. An Oregon line reported in 1904 that it was providing all its conductors "with standard accident release forms, it having been found that a signature can often be obtained on the spot, before a passenger has time to develop 'litigation symptoms.'" Some alighting accidents assumed a slightly eccentric character. In 1904 an Ohio

High water in 1907 and deep snow in 1912 were headaches on the Fort Dodge line. Flood waters more than a few inches deep stopped interurbans by shorting out the motors.

interurban lost an old lady passenger when, one evening, the car inadvertently ran past the place where she regularly got off. The car came to a halt on a trestle half a mile beyond. It was about to back up when, on the notion that she was at her stop, the grandmotherly old lady called out "Good night!" and backed down the steps in the darkness, plunging fatally off the trestle.

A somewhat similar accident was once heroically averted by a conductor named Brown on a New York interurban. As his car was accelerating away from a stop, Brown went to the passenger compartment to collect fares. Suddenly he saw a fragile old lady descending the rear steps under the nearsighted misapprehension that the car was still stationary. She was too far from Brown for him to grab in time, and much too deaf to hear his warning shout. So the conductor whipped out the front door of the then fast-moving car, miraculously keeping his footing, and caught the fragile old lady just as she toppled from the last step. She gravely thanked him for his assistance in descending.

One recurrent theme in the folklore of the interurban is the last-minute rescue of the toddler on the tracks, generally a golden-haired baby girl. This did actually happen on several lines, including the Rochester & Eastern in New York and the Lake Shore Electric in Ohio. In the latter instance, motorman William Lang was rocking along at about 55 when, close ahead, he spotted a child on the rails. Full emergency brakes weren't enough; he clambered agilely out on the shaky fender and on the run scooped up Leila Smith, aged two. Lang got a Carnegie lifesaving medal and a citation from President Theodore Roosevelt.

Several categories of interurban anecdote turn up often in employee reminiscences. When a trolley wheel jumped the wire at speed, the free pole often struck the supporting span wires violently. Sometimes it would rip loose the "overhead" and an energized wire would fall on the car roof, maybe snarling itself on a heater chimney or ventilator, arcing and sputtering with the ferocity of 600 volts at high amperage. If the wire snagged around the chimney there'd be a lurid display of flashing fireworks at the stove, but usually no harm beyond a minor fire or two. But if it should snarl the lavatory vent (a circumstance that has figured in many a story), any luckless passenger closeted inside would be subjected to appalling though probably not serious indignities.

The other oft-told story describes the new motorman on a third-rail line, too insufficiently schooled in his job to realize the preparations necessary before a trip, who felt an irresistible call of nature thirty minutes away from the terminal. His car was un-equipped for this, and he summoned his conductor urgently. The conductor counseled patience and future planning. This advice didn't suffice; in a few minutes the motorman abruptly stopped his car and nipped down the front steps in the darkness. Seconds later a wild cry out of the night betrayed that the young motorman had absentmindedly aimed too near to the third rail. The conductor and passengers found him stunned and, on revival, outraged, although otherwise undamaged.

Any number of oddities and mischances happened on interurbans. Several were held up by desperadoes in the best James brothers style. In 1912 an enterpris-ing band stopped three cars in one night not far from San Francisco, emptying the pockets of eighty pas-sengers and three conductors. (They were shortly nabbed on the Barbary Coast.) On an interurban near Geneva, New York, a stranger once confided to conductor Connie Ryan that he was an escaping con-vict. Could the conductor give counsel about the stop that was least likely to be watched by the police? Ryan and he considered the problem at length. The convict got off at the agreed-upon stop with a grateful wave, and Ryan called the police by the dispatching phone there.

A small boy was an interurban hero near Yakima, Washington, in 1932. Fishing earnestly beneath an interurban bridge with a thread and a bent pin, For-rest Johnson, aged nine, noticed that a freshet had washed out all support from beneath the rails at one span. Then he heard a hollow whistle in the distance and frenziedly scurried up the track, waving his red cap atop the fishing pole. In a perils-of-Pauline climax, he managed to stop a fast-moving car at the brink of the worthless bridge. Among other expres-sions of gratitude, the interurban company presented him with a de luxe fishing outfit.

In 1915 the Orange Limited was whizzing at 60 miles an hour toward Canandaigua, New York, when a passenger caught an imperfect glimpse of conductor George Ottley's heels disappearing out the rear win-dow. After pondering this remarkable image—the passenger wasn't really sure what he'd seen—he de-termined to report it to the motorman. They found Ottley some distance back, with a broken collarbone; he had been adjusting the trolley rope and had lost his balance.

An interurban was speeding rapidly across Ohio early one morning in 1907 when it crashed thunder-ingly into a solitary and deserted freight car sitting motionless on the tracks. The motorman was killed

and fire destroyed both cars. The perplexing question immediately arose as to where the mysterious car had come from. It couldn't have broken off a passing train—no freight had been along for days. It couldn't possibly have gotten there except by rail. It hadn't been there the evening before. Finally a solution came with a report that a car was missing from a siding on the far side of a town four miles away. There had been strong, gusty winds during the night, and evi-dently they had been enough to start the box car rolling when its brakes "leaked down." Late at night the car must have coasted spookily along the main

Rounding a curve, Philadelphia and Easton's No. 11 ran into a rock slide and derailed. Rerailing the car on the grade took laborious work with jacks and built-up cribbing.

street of the town, gliding to a stop miles out on the main line, awaiting its rendezvous.

The ambition and vitality of the interurban reached a kind of pinnacle in the Chicago-New York Air Line Railroad, a magnificent dream that flickered on and off from 1906 to about 1913. This was to have been a breathtaking piece of engineering and construction —a high-speed double track that was to stretch a direct 750 miles between the two cities, a distance hundreds of miles shorter than steam trunk lines required. It was to plunge through the Pennsylvania mountains in a series of dramatic tunnels and fills. There was to be no curve that couldn't be taken at

90 m.p.h., nor any grade greater than one-half of one per cent. Streamlined electric locomotives were to whisk luxurious cars between the cities in ten hours, indolently averaging 75 m.p.h. When in 1906 ground was first broken for construction of the road, thousands of Air Line stockholders felt that the world's most ambitious interurban would soon become the world's most profitable one too.

There were aspects of a crusade, or perhaps of a cult, about the Air Line. Each month stockholders received an exciting periodical, *The Air Line News*. It reported how wonderfully matters were progressing on the building of Your Railroad ("A huge Vulcan steam shovel is already on the job"). It printed pictures of steel girders that had already arrived for bridges; it ran enthusiastic letters from stockholders who had visited the site; and it carried coupons in each issue by which readers or their friends could apply for more stock, purchasable in installments.

In four or five sections of the country, Air Line stockholders formed into local clubs so they could get to know each other and could listen to speeches about their wonderful railroad. The land-acquisition program in Indiana, where construction took place, was also marked by an evangelical fervor. When Colonel Hord, the mellifluous and confidence-inspiring option man, approached even the most flinty-eyed farmer astride the right-of-way, the Colonel was quite likely to emerge with his option in his pocket, swapped for a few shares of stock, and sometimes with the farmer's savings as well, traded for a few extra shares.

The Air Line was not merely a hot-air promotion. Alexander C. Miller, the guiding spirit, J. D. Price, the president of the construction company, and their associates were substantial citizens with a background in railroading. Miller seems to have been a dedicated believer in the Air Line dream. If the com-

A freshly built interurban body, as recorded by a company photographer. Note the match-scratching plaques on the walls.

pany used high-pressure promotion methods, it was because conventional financing wouldn't serve for so grandiose a plan, and because banks were already heavily involved in competing interurbans. There seems to have been no hint of corporate sharp practices.

Nevertheless, a dismal sequence of troubles tarnished the shining dream. Enough stock was sold, on installments, to pay for the first 100-mile division east from Chicago. It was anticipated that as soon as this division began to make money, new investors would flock in to provide capital to build the other divisions. But a sharp business depression in 1907 and 1908 cut off the sale of stock, and brought widespread defaulting on installment payments for that already sold.

By the time money began to run out, some miles of main line had been constructed westward from a point outside La Porte, Indiana. The Air Line found itself in possession of some magnificent track that led, in terms of revenue traffic, from Nowhere to West Nowhere. Belatedly the company bent its efforts to build connecting links to nearby towns. It built an amusement park outside La Porte that generated some travel, and it fought fierce battles to obtain feeder franchises in Gary and elsewhere.

But the worst headache for the Air Line by far was the impractically high construction specifications. To keep within the maximum-grade limitation, each overpass that bridged a steam railroad had to be flanked by enormous ramps that started almost a mile on each side of the intersection. The Air Line actually built a number of these titanic embankments. Elsewhere across the gently rolling northern Indiana terrain, even minor undulations of the landscape created enormous difficulties. The worst trouble came

at a place called Coffee Creek, about a dozen miles from Gary. Here adherence to the specifications involved both a deep cut and a huge fill, 180 feet wide at the bottom, that marched for 2 miles across a valley. The power shovels and dump cars worked month after month at this grand undertaking, steadily pouring the stockholders' cash into a mound of earth of flabbergasting proportions.

Even though this crossing was ultimately completed, Coffee Creek helped kill the Air Line. By 1913 a kind of misshapen and unpromising interurban system was patched together between La Porte, Valparaiso, Gary, and Chicago. Less than 30 miles of it was dead-straight track built to Air Line standards, and the rest was ordinary, winding track. Among the cars operated by the company (which by then had no hope beyond that of surviving as a

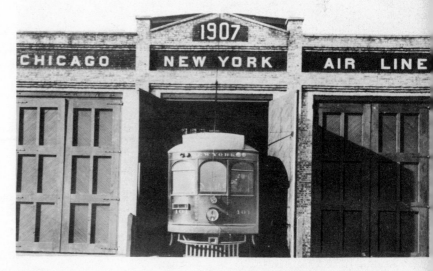

Cars No. 101 and 102 were the only first-line rolling stock that the Air Line had, but they were its prized possessions.

regional line) were two handsome Niles cars with NEW YORK lettered in gold on the eastern end and CHICAGO at the other. These two, and the stretches of arrowstraight track reaching toward the horizon, were what remained of the dream.

Interurban lines less beset by megalomania were in the same years humming with business. There was an unmistakably cocky quality about the big electric cars. It was reflected in the names given the de luxe runs: "The Crimson Limited," "The Wabash Flyer," "The Cannonball," "The Muncie Meteor." Name trains like these trundled out of town with ponderous arrogance, green flags socketed up front and a special signboard on the dash to show that this was no rustic local that stopped at every milk-loading platform and hamlet. This instead was a Limited, which demanded precedence all along the line. It offered parlor and buffet accommodations, stopped only at places of undoubted importance such as county seats, and provided the cleanest, fastest, most economical transportation a man could imagine. When you met a Limited on a city street you instinctively gave it plenty of room; even the throb of its air compressor sounded powerful and a little dangerous. In the country, where young farm children ran to the fence to see it rush by, it was capable of showing its contempt for all other transport by fragmenting a wagon or Model T with wrathful violence.

The Tacoma Limited trundled potently through Seattle streets.

Main Street of La Porte in 1913. The car shown belonged to a line that ran to Michigan City; the other rails here were the Air Line's link from La Porte to its straightaway main line.

A Western Ohio interurban easily towing two loaded trailers.

To the companies, interurban speeds were both a source of pride and a slight frustration. The difficulty lay in the time it took to get out of town, poking along behind city streetcars, held up by every one-horse rig that meandered along. Felix Reifschneider, a distinguished electric-car historian, once tabulated typical downtown-to-outskirts transit times as follows: Cleveland 45 minutes; Detroit, 45 minutes; Toledo, 20 minutes; Indianapolis, 25 minutes; and Buffalo, 30 minutes. Cars passing all the way through a town naturally spent much longer; a Cleveland-to-Detroit interurban might devote three-quarters of an hour to negotiating Toledo.

But once an interurban limited achieved its own right-of-way, speed was its proudest claim. Many a big Niles or Jewett car could travel along at a steady 65 or 70 miles an hour, and a few could touch 80 on places where the roadbed and overhead were smooth and true. Speed wasn't purely a matter of motors and gearing; there were various subtleties about the truck design on fast cars that lessened "nosing." (This was a distasteful and sometimes alarming oscillation that could develop at high speeds.) A number of interurban lines had stretches of track that paralleled steam-railroad track for a few miles. In the natural course

Easing into the street from its station, an interurban seemed huge and dangerous. Its right of way was rarely in dispute.

The great shed was just a part of the Indianapolis traction terminal. Some dozen different lines funneled into here.

of rivalry, this led to unofficial timetable modifications to permit occasional racing. Interurban motormen—there was an unsuccessful effort to christen them "motoneers"—were generally delighted when they could manage an informal race on these stretches with a steam "hog." It was particularly pleasant if the hogger wasn't alert enough to come chuffing into the stretch at a fast clip, because then he could almost invariably be "wiped" by the good performance of electric cars.

As the First World War neared, the interurban had won a place as an important part of the United States transportation system. There were 18,000 miles of interurban track in the country, almost half of it concentrated in the Middle West. Pennsylvania, New York, California, Massachusetts, and Texas, in that order, also had very considerable mileage. An immense sum of money, perhaps a billion dollars, was invested in interurban properties. In many cities the great sheds that served as interurban terminals were so bustling with activity that they quite matched the Union Stations of their steam rivals.

In 1904 there had opened in Indianapolis a traction terminal that soon grew to the biggest interurban center in the world. Within a decade it became so busy that 7 million passengers a year passed through it, and 500 interurban cars a day arrived or de-

One spot where interurbans and steam trains could race was a stretch of track between Uniontown and Fairchance, Pa.

parted. The freight load grew so heavy that the box cars had to be dispatched from a separate terminal, mainly sent out at night to keep from clogging the city streets with long strings of freight cars. As Indianapolis grew to be a wholesale business center for a large area, interurban companies boasted that within a radius of 75 miles deliveries could be promised on the same day that goods were ordered. (This, it should be noted, was still in a period when much of the citizenry held the view that a 75-mile trip was something a man might essay a few times in his life.)

As consolidation of the earlier small lines proceeded, long trips by interurban became technically possible. By hopping from system to system, a man could ride from Utica to Sheboygan, from Louisville to Bay City, from Grand Rapids to Cincinnati. As a rule only passengers with leisure took long trips, however, because steam trains were generally quicker or less roundabout for travel of more than 200 miles. But the interurban was often preferred for medium-distance and shorter trips, for here it usually offered

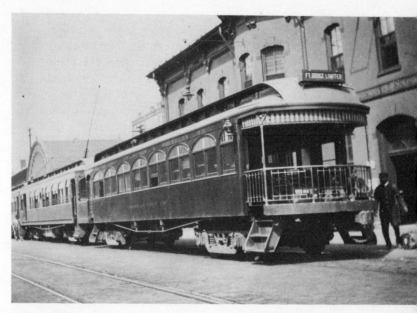

With an observation platform and porter service, this Fort Dodge Limited was travel de luxe.

Bucketing along at the road's edge, or flashing through a tunnel, the interurban symbolized speed and power to a generation of farm children. This was the Ohio Electric, near Zanesville.

faster or more frequent service. Women liked to come to town this way because they could get off right at the department stores; youngsters liked them because the cars were powerful and exciting; traveling salesmen liked them because they were companionable and cheap, and because they would stop right in front of the hotel, from which the porter would scurry out to take the sample cases.

By 1917, prosperous with new traffic swelling up from the approach of war, the big electric cars seemed at a peak of strength and vigor. To think otherwise then would have taken a special prescience—or at least an economist's brilliant analysis of the balance

sheets and annual reports. The omens, though, were there: a leveling-off in new trackage built (and most of that from consolidation); a sharp decline in new cars on order; a confused and spotty picture on passenger totals.

The cause of these ill omens and portents might well have seemed implausible then. For who could take seriously the ludicrous, wheezy flivvers, or the chain-driven, hard-tired trucks and buses? How was it possible to respect these slow and erratic contrivances when a kingly interurban, its whistle blowing, could scatter them so contemptuously at every crossing encounter?

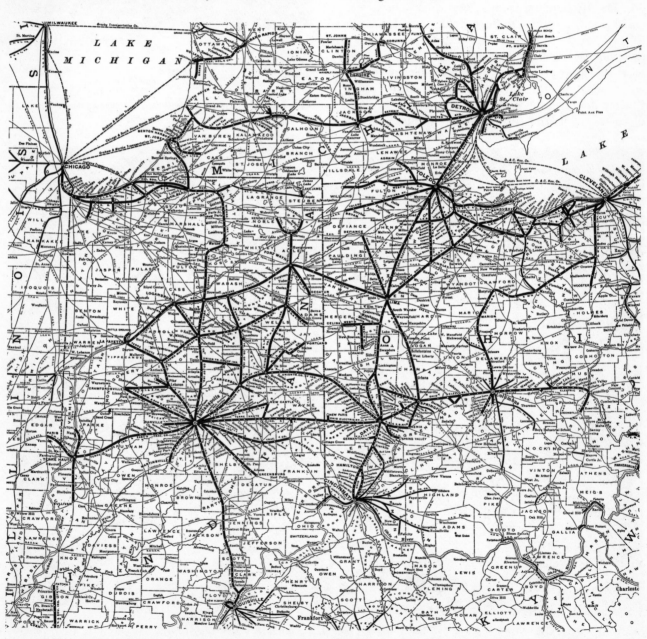

Some of the Midwestern interurban lines that operated in 1912.

9. THE GREAT YEARS

A conductor should never go inside the car without first counting the number of passengers on the rear platform; and if there are more there on his return, he should call out, "Fares, if you please," without addressing anyone in particular.

—Rule book for conductors

In the bright, morning-lighted years before the First World War, the image of an evil phenomenon called the "Trolley Trust" occurred to many Americans. It was a stylized image, one in which corpulent men, wearing silk hats and ascot ties embroidered with dollar signs, manipulated street railways for maximum personal profit and the greatest possible public inconvenience. A devil theory like this has always found an audience, and the trolley-trust notion was an entirely natural response to the Tarbell-Steffens climate. If there were pernicious and grasping trusts in oil, steel, and meat, and if corrupt municipalities were eager to barter franchises, what could be more likely than a vicious trolley trust?

The suspicion found reinforcement in the fact that almost everyone, at one time or another, became throbbingly angry at streetcars. It didn't take much; transportation is a peculiarly personal service. Crushed in a garlic-flavored rush-hour jam, or waiting interminably at a stop late some rainy night, or panting fruitlessly after some car that refused to stop, a man could easily perceive that his streetcar company was an evil and heartless conspiracy.

This was not an accurate perception. Watered stock was a kind of constitutional weakness with streetcar companies, it was true, and some managements were undoubtedly grasping above and beyond the call of free enterprise. A larger number of companies were simply trying to get along. A franchise *was* a kind of monopoly, to be sure, but a revocable one, with terms publicly recorded. Instead of being obtained by secret kickbacks, a franchise was more often secured by accepting municipal demands that the trolley company plow, sprinkle, and repave streets and pay taxes specially invented for the occasion. In Washington, D.C., a streetcar company was taxed to pay the wages of the traffic police; in Baltimore the company had to cough up 9 per cent of its gross revenues to maintain the public parks. While some men made a great deal of money from traction companies, they were persons whose finely honed instinct for gain would have allowed them to prosper at virtually anything.

Charles T. Yerkes, a man who by the nineties had assembled a streetcar empire in Chicago, and who was later deeply involved in London transit, did not depend on streetcars for his wealth. In his youth a shrewd broker, he dropped a fortune in the Chicago fire and then picked up another by contriving to be on the short side of the market in the Jay Gould panic. He was highly successful in that intricate game of chance known as the grain market. Henry Huntingdon of the Pacific Electric was another trolley millionaire who, at other times or places, would have prospered in furs, silks, ivory, or choice plots of land between Athens and Piraeus. In Philadelphia P. A. B. Widener in part built his fortune on horse-car consolidations, but he appears to have been guided by a shrewd, if not exactly benevolent, moderation.

Henry M. Whitney, the Boston magnate who had been so impressed by Sprague's Richmond installation, became involved in horsecars only by chance. He had prospered as a banker and president of his own shipping company. One day the notion struck him that it would be nice to unite his village of Brookline with Boston with a de luxe horsecar line. Very little would have come of it, in all probability, if an existing little horsecar line hadn't offended him by offering opposition. Opposition annoyed Whitney: he quickly bought control of a few decrepit horsecar lines, set them on their feet, gained control of others, merged them, and assembled in his West End Railway one of the biggest city transportation systems then in existence.

But though the devil theory of trolley finance may have been extreme, many a street railway helped it

Having a pan of flash powder fired off before his face was evidently more nerve-racking for Motorman Neut Russell than for his conductor and passengers. The car, which ran in Oil City, Pa., was a semiconvertible: the window sash could be slid upward into roof pockets to add breezes during hot weather.

This Philadelphia car shows the hollow curve to the sides that was inherited from the wheel-clearance needs of the old horse-drawn omnibus. But the shape was useful to trolleys in traffic, for inching by the hubs of drays and carriages.

along by assuming a corporate face of grimacing hostility. Writing in the *Electric Railway Journal* in 1914, Ivy Lee (a publicist who was later to earn fame for his success in rendering the elder Rockefeller palatable) advised companies to stop snarling at the public and start wooing it:

Electric railway managements are suffering from the same malady as that which afflicts the steam roads, namely, misunderstanding and distrust. Somehow the public has come to have the idea that three essential evils are embedded in the business:

1. That there is a vast amount of watered stock on which dividends are being paid.

2. That there is a widespread feeling that the railroads are ruled from Wall Street, that a small coterie of bankers in alliance with the so-called "money trust" is absorbing huge profits from the people.

3. That the railroads through their combinations of capital and management exercise undue power over the welfare of the people. With respect to electric railways there is often the feeling that this power is used locally against the welfare of the public.

An airy view from the back porch was a feature of this car, pictured at North Vassalboro, Maine. Observation platforms were rare except on interurbans in the Middle and Far West.

Six trolleys, gongs a-clanging, mix it up with horses, wagons, and pedestrians at an intersection in downtown Indianapolis.

Streetcar men stop at a spring for a sip of cool water on the Philadelphia streetcar system's Willow Grove line.

State militia fought pitched battles with several thousand striking motormen and conductors in Brooklyn in Jan., 1895. The strike, for $2 a day and a ten-hour day, was broken in two weeks; almost none of the strikers were rehired.

Lee's prescription was for warmer and less quarrelsome approaches toward the press and public. He might well also have counseled less flinty labor relations. A number of exceedingly bitter strikes by motormen and conductors took place in the early years of the century—acrimonious, prolonged, and often bloody. First the Knights of Labor and later the Amalgamated Association of Street Railway Employes fought a series of sharp campaigns for higher wages and a ten-hour day. The strikers rarely won, for companies generally waded in to meet the conflict head-on, if necessary with the assistance of the police, the militia, and private organizations that specialized in supplying professional strikebreakers. Public exasperation at interruptions of service soon overcame natural sympathy for the strikers. When conductors and motormen jerked off the trolley poles of cars brought out of the carbarns by strikebreakers, Donnybrooks usually took place— with broken glass, cracked skulls, paddy-wagonfuls of strikers, and agitated newspaper editorials of the this-lawlessness-must-cease variety.

When these old battles were viewed from the softening perspective of time, it seems evident that individual strikers often made out best when gangs of professional strikebreakers were imported and the strike was promptly smashed. One reason for this paradox was that even a lost strike soon won some concessions. Another was that professional strikebreakers were rarely willing to accept permanent employment, so that after tempers had simmered down, most of the original conductors and motorman got their jobs back. Where the company fought back with locally hired replacements, and where the struggle was long and bitter, blacklisting of the strikers remained effective for years.

Considering the wages commonly paid, conductors and motormen had legitimate discontents. In Philadelphia in 1903 they received 20¢ an hour, working six 10½-hour days for $12.60. They bought their uniforms from the company at $10 apiece, of which $1.60 was company profit. In New York City then, conductors and motormen of highest seniority could make about thirteen or fourteen dollars a week, provided they were willing to work a seven-day week. What particularly rankled here was that this was only about half the wages earned by policemen and firemen of equivalent seniority; and just as streetcar officials liked to be thought of as railroaders, motormen and conductors liked to feel they were the social equals of the police and firemen.

Away from the large cities, wages were lower. On a Rockford, Illinois, interurban line in 1903, the starting wage for a motorman or conductor was fourteen cents an hour. This progressed with seniority up to a maximum of eighteen cents an hour, for those who had worked six or more years. Each Christmas on this line, motormen who had gone all year without having any accident at all received a special award of ten dollars. By the standards of the time, these wage scales were of course not as niggardly as they seem now. But they were also neither remotely liberal nor in scale to the responsibilities of the jobs.

With wages so low, the temptation for a conductor to help himself to a few fares—usually by collecting them but not ringing them up on the register—was virtually irresistible. If a twelve-dollar-a-week conductor making ten round trips a day could manage to pocket an average of just one nickel per half trip, he could boost his weekly take-home pay 50 per cent. The path by which an honest conductor might be led into "peculation" was broad and easy, as the *Street Railway Journal* observed:

The present system tends to make conductors dishonest. A strictly honest man begins work today. He is 80 cents over. He turns it in. Tomorrow he is 60 cents over and turns that in. The third day 40 cents. Now the office calls him in and tells him he must be more careful to ring up all fares. He tries, but finds himself 35 cents over the following day. To turn it in again is to be subject to criticism for inefficiency. "If I keep this up I lose my job, may be," is his natural inference. He pockets the over. All is smooth now, so he continues to keep his overs. From this point to a habit of neglecting rings to increase overs is an easy transition. He started honest, but the company taught him that it was precarious, so now he fortifies his efficiency and swells his purse.

On larger trolley systems chronic warfare developed between light-fingered conductors and plainclothes company spotters. Ingenious tricks were practiced on each side. The commonest—and crudest—conductor technique was to collect fares from six or seven people, and then ring up a tattoo on the register that was one fare short. A subtler version was to collect fares just before the car came to a stop, when a conductor had to hurry to the back platform to signal the start. Once the car was under way again, he would ring up all but one of the fares previously collected. A third procedure was to ring up every fare inside the car with conspicuous precision, but to manage to miss a few standees crammed on the rear platform. A nameless genius discovered that, on one type of fare register, there was an exciting flaw of design. If the register cord was not quite fully released after ringing up a fare, a subsequent tug on the cord

The car waiting by the Indiana State Prison, presumably not for escapees, is a convertible. In the summer its sides were taken off and the folded footboard swung down for a step.

A wayside stop outside Franklin, Pa. The notice on the shed offered a liberal reward for the conviction of persons found guilty of breaking the traction company's lamp bulbs.

Twelve tracks led into the lavish brick carbarn of the Citizens Traction Company at Oil City, Pa. Spare ties and poles for the overhead wire were stacked up in readiness outside.

These docile and self-conscious passengers posed in 1912 to show the interior arrangement of the new "nearside" cars.

would ring the bell but not advance the counter. A man with a deft touch on the cord could produce three juicy rings for only two fares added to the counter total.

Some streetcar companies provided hand registers, commonly known as "guns." These were the small mechanisms that conductors proffered to passengers for the insertion of fares, and they seemed to be theft-proof. But they weren't. The trick was to buy or rent an extra gun on the black market, where lost, stolen, or bootlegged hand registers could be had. All nickels that went through the company gun were meticulously turned in, and all that passed through the private gun were pocketed. It was usually the practice to keep a private gun hidden out somewhere along the route, safely away from the carbarn.

Motormen could also take a hand in the nickel game. When a new conductor showed no enthusiasm for "knocking down" and sharing lunch money, a tough motorman might regularly bring the trip in off its schedule, earning repeated reprimands on the new conductor's record until his job was in jeopardy. Once he had the new man in trouble with the company, the motorman might point out that with a little

cooperation, the car *could* make its schedule better. He'd further point out how a crafty motorman was a good partner at "fare play." Along the crowded part of a trip, the motorman would lay behind schedule, picking up every possible passenger. Once through the downtown area, the motorman would run much faster than usual, to get to the end of the line on schedule. The slight excess of passengers this produced meant that a conductor could knock off fares and still turn in receipts of average size. It could also be worked in reverse when a motorman suspected that his conductor wasn't divvying fairly. He'd "run close to his leader" and pass by would-be riders, giving his conductor both lean pickings and disquietingly low receipts to turn in.

Unexpected pitfalls awaited young conductors without natural aptitude for petty larceny. One harrowing tale has been confided by a man now swathed in respectability:

I worked for a year as a youngster on an upstate trolley line. The pay was extremely small, and very gradually I fell into the habit of clipping the company pretty hard. Nobody knew anything about it, and things went smoothly. Then one morning I woke up with a bad

Gilt decorations reflected company pride in its rolling stock.

The sinuous path of the tracks here wasn't pure whimsy; they had to climb enough, in close quarters, to clear a railroad line beneath. Taken about 1908, at Wiconisco, Pa.

cold. I was about to report sick when it belatedly dawned on me that I couldn't possibly risk taking a day off. The receipts on my runs would show a sudden, eloquent increase. So I dragged off to the carbarn, wheezing and coughing, and spent weeks in tapering my take down to the point where I could indulge in the luxury of being sick. My cold was all gone by then, but my chills weren't.

Timid conductors who lacked confidence in their ability at brazenly underringing the register were prospective customers for a "brother-in-law." This was an extraordinary cheating machine, one that was viewed with amused superiority by crafty old hands, and that was avoided by those who realized that its possession was prima facie evidence of an intent to steal. It still had great appeal to novice underringers. It consisted of a clockwork mechanism worn under a conductor's coat, usually strapped in the left armpit like a shoulder holster. A catgut string ran down his left sleeve and was looped inconspicuously around a finger. When the finger was straightened, the clockwork made a fine ringing noise, identical with that of the register. A conductor gathering in a fare need only reach up toward the register cord, pull it ineffectually, and simultaneously twitch a finger. The

Trestles and tunnels added spice to open-car rides in West Virginia. This car was on a viaduct over Mitchell Hollow.

brother-in-law would emit a plausible "Kaa-chingg!" and another nickel would be in hand.

The transfer was a notion that contributed considerably to the growth of city streetcar systems. Although transfers helped to keep passenger totals climbing steeply in the first decade and a half of this century, they had curiously tough sledding at first.

In the form of undated brass checks, they had limited use in horsecar days. But the general custom then, when separate lines were typically owned by separate companies, was to offer just one ride for one fare. By the mid-nineties, so many consolidations of trolley lines had taken place that the notion of permitting riders to change to other routes began to be put forward. It was argued that if you made trolley riding more useful to people, more people would ride. Conservative managements opposed it steadfastly at first, except where the transfer privilege was so hedged with restrictions as to be practically valueless. What on earth was the sense of giving away something that you might get paid for?

It turned out that there was a great deal of sense

Riding an open car to Hartford in 1900 was a pleasure, for it rolled smoothly along handsome, tree-shaded village streets.

Off-hour schedules usually gave a car crew a few minutes of loafing time at the end of the track. Boone, Iowa, in 1911.

Binghamton R. R. Co.
TRANSFER.
Good only for this current trip,
from point of transfer, on next car — 40 +
over the line punched after time canceled. Subject to Rules of Company.
☞ PICTURE PUNCHED INDICATES TYPE OF PASSENGER.
TRADE-MARK,
Issued by
Conductor No.   **47**

1	1 2 3 4 5
2	1 2 3 4 5
3	1 2 3 4 5
4	1 2 3 4 5
5	1 2 3 4 5
6	1 2 3 4 5
7	1 2 3 4 5
8	1 2 3 4 5
9	1 2 3 4 5
10	1 2 3 4 5
11	1 2 3 4 5
12	1 2 3 4 5

| 1 | 2 | 3 | 4 | 5 | 6 | 7 | 8 | 9 | 10 | 11 | 12 | 13 | 14 | 15 |
| 16 | 17 | 18 | 19 | 20 | 21 | 22 | 23 | 24 | 25 | 26 | 27 | 28 | 29 | 30 | 31 |

MANUFACTURED BY GLOBE TICKET COMPANY PHILADELPHIA, PA.

X	X	ROSS	VILLE	LESTER	SHIRE	ASY	LUM
O	HOME	GLEN	WOOD	P. DICK	INSON	DEP	OTS
C	C	WEST	MAIN	NO. CHE	NANGO	S.FO	REST
		BROAD	AVE	LEROY	STREET		

IF BLACK PORTION PUNCHED TIME IS P. M.

in it. By 1903 the *Street Railway Journal* was advising:

Today there are few men in the profession who do not know of their own knowledge that giving transfers is the most lucrative thing that the street railways ever hit upon for the increase of business and cash receipts. Transfers not only induced people to ride, but they taught them to ride—they made riding a habit.

The miracle wrought by the transfer reads like a fairy tale. Not only have the receipts of main lines been doubled and trebled under its magic influence, but subsidiary lines that were either dead or dying have been transformed into paying investments of the first rank. No other development in street-railway traffic can be compared for a moment to this.

Inevitably, growing pains accompanied the perfecting of workable transfer systems. It soon became evident that transfer points had to be carefully located, because the transfer-passenger load, pumped

into an intersecting line at a place where the second line was already hard-pressed, could snarl traffic savagely. This brought tricky problems in dispatching: a route might warrant only so many cars per hour up to a point where it hit a transfer intersection, and then need far more cars per hour beyond that spot.

There were other troubles. People displayed a strong impulse to try to use transfers for stopover purposes; a woman would want to ride downtown, get off with a transfer, do her errands, and then use the transfer to go elsewhere. Many a rider, impelled by cloudy notions of getting his money's worth, made a point of invariably collecting a free transfer, needed or not. Alert urchins found that cadging these unneeded transfers from alighting passengers and retailing them, at two cents apiece, to boarding ones was a profitable piece of free enterprise. Sometimes people coming into offices and stores would deposit unneeded transfers in an informal exchange, from which others might select something useful.

Some early efforts to control these misuses were fanciful. In Minneapolis and elsewhere, transfers were printed that bore seven little line-drawing portraits of typical passengers, generally five men of varying whiskeriness, and two women in different hats. The issuing conductor was supposed to put a punch mark next to the face most nearly resembling that of the passenger, the theory being that a man wearing Dundreary whiskers, for example, would thus be discouraged from presenting a transfer

People could pour off an open car in a hurry at a common destination. This was at the Brighton Beach, N.Y., race track.

punched for a matron in a bonnet. Other lines, wary of this physiognomic approach, tried elaborate color and letter codes, special validating punches, and long lists of prohibitions printed on each transfer. In a few cities the problem of creating an abuse-proof transfer system appeared so difficult that the alternative was tried of building closed-in stations where people could walk from car to car. But this was awkward, expensive, and unpopular with riders. "The public," one trolley superintendent noted with detachment, "don't like to be herded into a pen or corral."

By 1905 reasonably workable transfer systems had been developed. Stopover shoppers and transfer exchanges were countered by establishing a ten- or fifteen-minute life to a transfer, as evidenced by a punched time limit on a printed clock dial, or by tear-off time coupons. The same measure, aided by

a little police pressure, helped to curb the urchin-entrepreneurs. So also did the occasional practice of issuing transfers only for a two-cent premium. Traffic surveys helped unravel the snarls created by transfer loads. In the ceaseless battle against light-fingered conductors, transfer skulduggery was kept under control by such steps as serially numbering transfers and giving conductors punches that made individually identifiable marks.

So the cars rolled on and the passengers poured in, drawn in swelling numbers by the fine new utility that transfers gave trolleys.

Trolleys have always had an affinity for peculiar accidents. In 1906 a ridiculous mishap nearly bankrupted a small Ontario interurban. Snows too deep for ordinary plows and sweepers were repeatedly delaying its service. There was no money for an expensive rotary plow that could slice its way through the

Small parades had to squeeze over to let the trolleys go by. The gala occasion here took place in Asbury Park, N.J.

Lunch stop for a snowplow crew in 1916. A separate motor spun a rotary's blades, and chutes directed the discharged snow.

More than a dozen trolleys disputed with countless horse-drawn vehicles when this view of Market St. in Newark, N.J., was taken about 1909. But there was not an auto in sight.

drifts, slinging the snow aside. The superintendent, who wanted a rotary so badly that he dreamed of it, begged the company officers for one until they finally gave in and scratched up the cash. When the shiny plow arrived the super was like a youngster at Christmas. He left strict orders with the night dispatcher to call him at the first sign of a heavy snow. The call came at three on a blizzardy morning and the super hurried to the carbarn and rode out at the controller of the new plow. The rotary munched its way without a halt through every drift to the far end of the line. There, though, an agitated message from the dispatcher was waiting. The super had forgotten to adjust the discharge lever when clanking down the main street of one town. His wonderful new plow had hurled the wet snow aside with such vigor as to smash in the front windows of houses all along the street, piling the parlors within with melting snow.

A trolley once perplexingly vanished for a few hours in Waterbury, Connecticut. The line was a dead-ended single track, and routines prescribed that each outbound car should wait at a turnout several miles from the end of the line until its "leader" came back in the opposite direction. One night the returning car didn't show up. After a long wait, the motor-

The signal on the pole told a motorman whether he could go beyond a passing turn-out on a single-track section of line.

Over the bank but upright, this Vermont car posed a problem.

If derailed at speed, a trolley might lunge off ferociously. This one went house-hunting in Connecticut on Dec. 10, 1904.

man at the turnout decided that the missing car must have broken down. He proceeded cautiously to the very end of the line without catching a glimpse of it. Baffled, he changed trolley poles, flipped the seats, loaded a few waiting passengers, and started back to town. The explanation emerged later that night at the end of the line, after the last passenger from an owl car had walked off. A somewhat shamefaced man emerged from the shadows, identified himself as the missing motorman, and asked his colleague if he knew where they could borrow a *really* long tow rope. He explained that, all alone in his car, he had absently gone careening off the end of the track at full speed. His trolley had veered off the road, crossed a field, and then had come to rest embedded deeply in some thick brush. He'd walked back to the rails' end to ask for help, but had felt too embarrassed to identify himself as long as there were any passengers around.

In all the history of trolleys perhaps no accident was as bizarre as the mischance that befell a Massachusetts streetcar on September 21, 1904. A car from Boston was rolling along an elm-lined street in the town of Melrose with 32 passengers aboard. It was a dark evening; the street lights were off because the town had a "moonlight schedule"—a thrifty habit of saving electricity when the moon was near full. There seems a possiblity that motorman Winfield Rowe may have glimpsed a wildly waving figure running toward him, 100 yards away. No one will ever know, though, because in the next instant Rowe and many of his passengers were dead or dying. The front half of the trolley blew to bits in a tremendous spouting explosion that flung fragments and bodies high up in the elms. A 50-pound box of dynamite had been lying on the tracks, where it had fallen a few mo-

ments before from the tailgate of an express wagon. The expressman had discovered his loss and had come running back for the box. But the trolley got there first, and 13 people died.

A revolutionary change in car design was tried for the first time in Montreal in 1905. This was a "PAYE" car, forerunner of a new kind of city trolley. To streetcar companies the PAYE idea—the term came from the initials of the phrase Pay As You Enter—was highly seductive. It promised more revenue from the same passenger loads and more efficient passenger handling within the car. With even the most conscientious and photographic-memoried conductors, virtues that managements felt were all too rare at best, a considerable percentage of passengers were believed to ride for nothing. In rush hours particularly it was very difficult for a conductor making his way along the aisle to be sure who'd paid and who hadn't, so that fare collection lapsed into a kind of disheveled honor system, with overtones of poker playing.

PAYE cars were to correct all this. Fewer people could get by without paying if they were expected to cough up a nickel before they had a chance to "mingle deceptively" with other riders. The increased receipts, moreover, would be pure velvet, achieved without increasing service or adding to labor costs. Conductor larceny would be harder to perform, and easier to detect. Accidents would lessen with one of the crew always on station at each end of a car. Fewer passengers would inadvertently be asked to pay their fares twice, and with alighting riders standing close to the motorman they would be less likely

To the acute embarrassment of the rookie employee who was putting No. 532 in the North Abington, Mass., carbarn, the willful car kept going until it crashed right out the rear wall.

Ice-laden trolley wires fell on and electrocuted this team.

This was among the first PAYE cars to win a trial in Chicago.

to be carried past their stops—eliminating two major causes of loud and angry scenes.

For a wonder, most of these anticipated benefits came to pass. Receipts did go up; "peculations" did slope down; and the safety record was improved. The PAYE system soon won wide acceptance. It wasn't adapted to side-loading open cars, of course, and it offered no particular advantages in interurbans with their relatively infrequent stops. On city lines, though, prepayment cars soon had it all over their predecessors, which became known as "Pay-the-Old-Way" cars.

As always with trolleys, there turned out to be headaches. Increased loading time was by far the worst. A streetcar neither makes money nor pleases its customers while it stands motionless; its natural and profitable condition is trundling onward. When in the rush hour a large clutch of passengers attempted to swarm aboard the rear of an early PAYE car, interminable delays developed. People with large parcels would plunk them down in the doorway while exploring vest pockets for elusive transfers. Persons who suddenly found themselves getting on the wrong car would elbow their way off against the flow. Women would rummage through their reticules in leisurely pursuit of a nickel. Signs and the conductor's chant, *Have-your-fare-ready-Step-lively-Have-your-fare-ready,* were tried as correctives, without much result.

It became evident that cars would have to be specially designed for PAYE operation. The trick was to enlarge the area of the rear platform until it could hold a goodsized batch of boarders, including all the fumblers likely to get aboard at a single stop. A conductor could then signal the car forward the moment everyone was aboard, subsequently collecting from the slowpokes on the platform. This worked fairly well after people grew accustomed to the new system.

A second drawback resulted from the solution to

A spacious rear platform let fumblers dig for fares en route.

A PAYE front platform, gathering place for firemen and cops.

Departing riders debarked with grace from the front platform.

the first problem: cars with extra-large rear platforms were not suitable for double-ended operation. At the end of the line it was not enough to flip the seats and change trolley poles; now the car itself had to be physically turned around. This meant turn-around trackage, either a loop or a wye. (The latter, shaped like the letter Y, is a stub track into which a car can be moved and then headed back out in an opposite direction.)

Several new internal car arrangements grew popular. One was the Peter Witt car, named after a Cleveland street-railway commissioner, in which the conductor was stationed in the center of the car to supervise two side doors. Peter Witts were often called "Pay-As-You-Pass cars." The entire front half was a sort of internal platform or payment area. A rider could either drop his fare in the box and walk to the rear of the car, later leaving by the "rear center door," or else pay as he departed by the "front center door." Peter Witts proved to be highly efficient, and especially good on congested lines.

A variant of this, the nearside car, was the special favorite of T. E. Mitten, head of the firm that operated lines in Buffalo, Philadelphia, and Chicago. In a nearside car, passengers both boarded and departed by a large front door, and the conductor, functioning

mainly as a cashier, was stationed close behind the motorman. Later modification of many nearsides added a center door for departures. The name came from the practice in some cities of locating stops on the near side of an intersecting street; front-entrance cars were believed better for nearside stops, rear-entrance cars better for farside stops. Beginning in 1911, Philadelphia in particular took nearsides to its heart; 1,500 of them were running there in two years. (The last one clanked to a halt in 1955.)

Under the pressure of steadily rising passenger totals, trolley companies endlessly experimented with car design. Some basic economic and physical laws grew clearer. One was that it wasn't smart to try to cope with peak loads simply by putting on more cars, because this ran the "platform charge"—the labor cost—way up. It was wiser to handle as much of the peak as possible by using bigger cars. The platform charge being a major expense, a company obviously made more money by increasing loading than by increasing the number of crews at work.

At the same time, it grew evident that there was much more to a good car than pure capacity. Quick-loading, fast-accelerating cars were desirable, not particularly because they pleased the customers, but because they gave more service, in relation to crew

Nearside cars at first stationed the conductor up front behind the motorman, to act as combined cashier and doorkeeper.

labor, than slower cars. As early as the mid-nineties, the single-truck four-wheelers had begun to show a serious limitation. If in the effort to gain capacity the wheelbase was stretched out too much, the car wouldn't negotiate sharp curves; if the wheelbase was left alone and the body extended in overhang, the car tended to lollop along in an unpleasing canter, and to derail on slight provocation. So double-truck cars took over because they could be made much longer and still manage small-radius curves—the critical wheelbase being that of the trucks, not the distance between trucks.

By the time PAYE forced further modification in car design, it was plain that cars needed to be bigger still, carrying more passengers in relation to the crew. They needed to start and stop faster, and to have the fewest possible bottlenecks to restrict passenger movement. Mounting lawsuits suggested that cars should also have gates or doors that could physically retain the people who had wedged themselves aboard, and that could exclude frenzied late arrivers. Women's clothes, too, grew to be a problem in 1912,

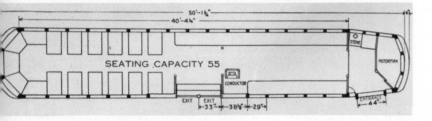

Peter Witt cars, named after the Cleveland traction commissioner who designed them, used the entire front half of the car for the temporary storage of unpaid passengers. From here they either paid and sat down, or paid and got off.

Bogus accidents were once photographed to dramatize the virtues of the front exit on nearside cars. Departing riders from ordinary cars, it was gloomily suggested, could find many ways to come to grief when crossing in the rear.

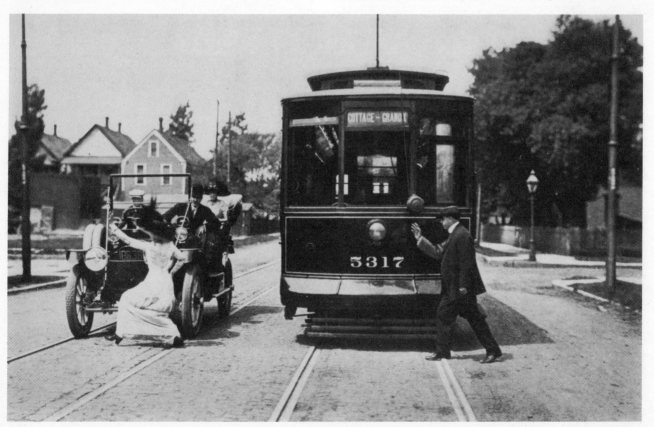

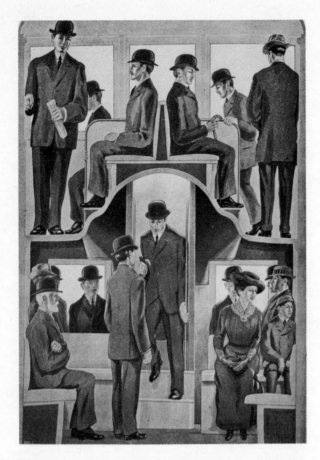

Derisively called the "Broadway Battleship," No. 6000 in New York City was an experimental double-decker with a low hobble-skirt side door. It didn't prove to be successful.

when the rage for a peculiar garment called the hobbleskirt spread across the country. If trigged out in a smart hobbleskirt, a lady who attempted to scale a high, two-step platform needed considerable time, several male hands at the elbows, or a derrick.

In New York, Pittsburgh, and elsewhere, there was periodic experimentation with double-deckers. These could absorb impressive volumes of humanity but they were expensive to build and they invited stairway accidents. Worse, they were very sluggish at loading and unloading. In many cities trailer cars were tried with better luck, motorless cars that could be towed along during the rush hour by regular cars. Another promising expedient was the trolley train—two or even three cars coupled together and operated by multiple-unit control. Acceleration wasn't reduced as it might be with trailer cars. A conductor was needed in each car, of course, so that the platform charge wasn't held down ideally. Still a three-car trolley train had an operating crew of four, as opposed to the six that would have been needed by the same cars run separately. The hobbleskirt problem was initially grappled with by the Los Angeles Railway—on the realistic concept that it was much simpler to change wood and steel than women's fashions—when it brought out the first depressed-center, middle-loading car, with a platform just one low step off the ground.

It remained for Boston to cook up in 1913 a par-

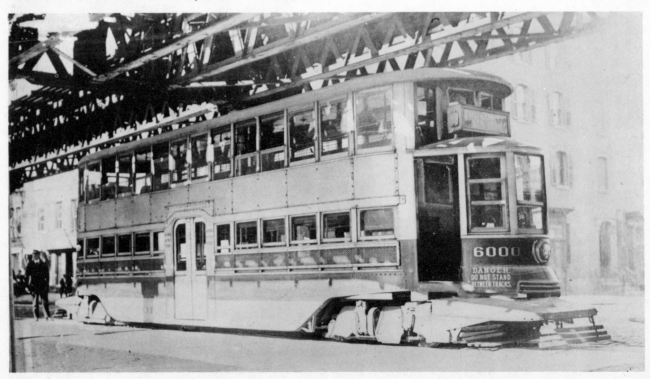

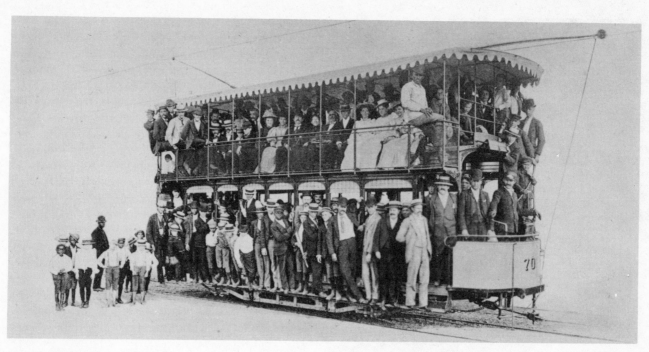

Traction officials liked the idea of double-deckers: so many fares could be packed aboard. Though often tried, they were found to be slow loaders. Tipping over of a double-decker, though feared by the anxious, was a rare event.

Snake-dancing through Harvard Square in Sept., 1912, No. 405 was Boston's first "two rooms and a bath" car. Later ones of the species used two double-truck cars.

simonious Yankee variant that seemed to cope with every problem in sight. The Boston Elevated Railway took pairs of obsolete cars and joined them to little central compartments. This internal caboose had no wheels of its own; it was suspended by both cars, and flexibly connected so that the entire rig could snake around Boston's narrow streets. The conductor and his fare box were stationed in the middle, behind large air-operated doors. Seen from the side, the car vaguely resembled a rubbery-kneed drunk supported by two stalwart friends; most Bostonians, preferring a more decorous image, fell into the habit of referring to it as "two rooms and a bath." These articulated cars won the company's heart, both by giving new life to outdated rolling stock and by carrying twice the passenger load for each crew. Loading time was quite good, too, because the passengers streaming aboard could veer to either the right or left, whichever was the less crowded. A fleet of "two rooms" was soon running, with such success

"Plenty of room forward," a conductor would chant, breasting the rush-hour torrents. A Cleveland center-entrance car.

that by 1917 the company began buying new cars designed around "two rooms" principles. The new ones gave up the articulated idea, being created from scratch, but they were big center-entrance cars with low platforms, proportioned so that they could gobble or spew out people at a tremendous rate. By 1921 Boston had nearly 500 of these behemoths, and when run in trains of three they were veritable crowd-swallowers. Some of the original "two rooms," incidentally, stayed in service until 1924, startling visitors to the city with their flexibility as they writhed along.

The rush hour, a major operating headache on practically all city systems, supplied intense pressure for car improvement. It seemed to grow worse every year and was the bane of every trolley superintendent's life. Nothing exasperated a super more than newspaper editorials suggesting that the rush hour was enjoyably lucrative for a trolley company. Actually the rush hour was expensive and wasteful, a diffi-

cult obstacle in the way of efficient operation. A company had to invest in cars, generating capacity, distribution wires, carbarns, and a hundred other things that were scaled for the rush hour, even though this costly equipment was needed for only three hours out of twenty-four. Conductors and motormen couldn't be expected to work only three hours a day, which meant that work schedules had to be used that provided too many crews for part of the time and too few for other periods. More accidents happened in the rush hour. More electricity per car mile was used up, because motormen had less chance to run on the higher, more economical controller points. More breakdowns and stoppages occurred then, and brake shoes and wheels wore out faster. As a crowning frustration, people tended to move in great tidal currents during the rush hour, which meant that cars traveling in one direction were overloaded while the cars coming back were wastefully unoccupied.

For street-railway men, the exciting years before

Jam-packed streets could magnify the rush-hour frustrations.

1917 posed only the problems of success—of mounting passenger totals, record gross incomes, steadily climbing trackage. There were clouds on the horizon, for those who liked to worry, but to many trolley men they seemed no bigger than a man's hand. Sometimes the pessimists talked about intractable costs, or new shapes to the growth curves, or the noisier chug of the flivvers. No matter—hadn't trolleys always been beset by problems, many more serious than these, and hadn't they always won out?

For proof it was the fashion to cite the tremendous rail network that had sprung up in and between cities in the United States. Long-distance trips by trolley were now possible. Many companies advertised the idea of trolley-tour vacations—leisurely, rambling tours that provided an incomparably close view of both city and countryside. One favorite trip,

taken by many an early trolley fan, involved riding between New York and Boston solely by streetcar. The total fare for this 267-mile jaunt was $3.75, and the actual running time was eighteen hours and eight minutes, to which had to be added any time spent waiting for connections and eating. By 1913 it was almost possible to make a far longer trip, one of breathtaking dimensions. It ran more than 1,000 rail miles from Waterville, Maine, to Sheboygan, Wisconsin. It would have taken more than a week, with about 150 hours of actual riding time. But a pair of 20-mile gaps in New York State were never closed, and no one ever made the trip purely by trolley.

It was a pity that no company had the vitality to close those little gaps, if only for a short time. Because in the years that were immediately ahead, it was not the trackage that was to grow, but the gaps.

A favorite scenic ride in the east was along the Delaware Water Gap.

10. THE RIDE DOWNHILL

At the beginning of the twentieth century, a development took place which was to have a marked effect not only on street railways, but on all forms of transportation. Horseless vehicles had been talked about for years, but few people even dreamed the effect they would have on our future social life.

—President of a traction company

About 4 million Americans regularly rode bicycles in 1896. The craze worried many streetcar officials. Endowed with normal amounts of self-interest, they warily eyed this strange national mania for two-wheelers. It was, after all, a rival method of transportation, and one that had sprung up almost overnight. A bicycle was cheaper than a horse and rig, it could be stored away very easily, and it took a man exactly where he wanted to go. There was evidence that bicycles had actually cut into traffic totals on certain streetcar lines. Who could say how far this alarming fad might develop?

In a few years the anxiety abated. Trolley men theorized that the skill demanded of a bicyclist was actually too great for a successful system of mass transportation, blissfully unaware that trolleys were ultimately to be done in by something that needed far greater operating skill. When in time it grew obvious that bicycling was to a considerable degree a social phenomenon and a sport, and that people in the greatest numbers would prefer not to pump their legs to get about, streetcar executives turned their watchful eyes upon the horseless carriage.

It was difficult just after the turn of the century for even the most dour and pessimistic railway man to regard the automobile seriously. To most people this rare vehicle was irresistibly comic. It shivered and popped, wheezed and exploded, when it did anything at all. Costing a great deal and behaving badly, it was a proper possession of the eccentric rich. Still, an almost prophetic edginess can be discerned in the first auto references in the electric-railway press. Massachusetts was warmly applauded for requiring in 1903 the registration of "chauffeurs," with the tart observation that trolleys were rarely known to depart unidentified from the scene of an accident. Often the comment was one of annoyance at the way wealthy autoists ignored the speed limits that trolleys had been held to. Said a 1902 editorial:

Why should our plutocratic contemporary who drives his Devouring Dragon 50 miles an hour over the public roads be exempt from the same speed limits enforced against the trolley? The latter is a public convenience, the former a public nuisance. Competition is trivial now, but if a coterie of wealthy scorchers, with big pulls, gets the bars down in the matter of speed, they will never go up again. It is well to kill snakes before they get a chance to grow fangs.

The automobile continued to twang upon trolley nerves. In 1904 the *Street Railway Journal* published a long essay on the future of the automobile. Intended to be a counsel of good cheer, it began moderately but became steadily angrier and ended with a baleful red glare of a man who has just bashed his thumb with a hammer:

It must at the start be recognized that the devil wagon has come to stay. It contains the elements of great practical usefulness, and while thus far developed in a scatter-brained sort of way, is certain sooner or later to enter upon a stage of sound growth. . . .

We are not inclined to share the roseate view of those who hold that the world will enter upon an automobile era, in which a swarm of devil wagons will fill the highways. In the nature of things the automobile must continue to be a costly machine. . . . The question of money is likely to keep automobiles from being a serious factor in rapid transit. . . .

The particular danger to transit interests in the automobile craze lies not in legitimate competition but in unfair discrimination. The whole headstrong crew of automobile scorchers, caring absolutely nothing for the rights of others upon the public roads, are using every effort to have all restrictions upon speed removed. If private vehicles run unmolested at 25 or 30 m.p.h., then what is to hinder an automobile omnibus line from doing

York Beach, Maine, early in the century. Neither horse-drawn rigs nor costly autos threatened the capable trolleys.

A Pacific Electric trolley loomed big by a horseless carriage.

More and more autos came to share the streets. Red Bank, N.J.

Brass headlight rims gleaming, new autos were far more exciting than streetcars. This was downtown Newark in 1907.

the same thing, and if such speed is legalized, which is the constant effort of the scorchers, then a new weapon will be put in the hands of the swine who desire the "common people," who use street cars, to take to the back alleys, while they, the self-chosen elect, pre-empt the streets. . . .

Although it may have been keen intuition that made streetcar men irritable about the auto, there was for more than a decade no clear-cut threat of a sort to alarm experienced streetcar superintendents. The prevailing view, in fact, was somewhat complacent. Every year trolley-riding totals reached more

In 1912 this contraption ran in Laurel Canyon, Los Angeles.

The earliest Fifth Avenue buses showed their overseas origin.

astronomical figures. The better streetcar securities were the gilt-edged aristocrats among all utility stocks and bonds, and what class of men were more practiced at scanning the future than investment bankers? The most urgent trolley problems were not those of competition but of expansion to meet demand, and of controlling a surge in costs. No real rivalry, beyond a few piffling upstart enterprises, could be anywhere seen.

From 1905 on, to be sure, a gasoline-powered bus line was actually carrying people commercially in America. This was the Fifth Avenue Coach Company in New York City, which began service that year with lumbering, solid-tired hybrids—double-decked bodies built in the United States by Brill, perched on engines and chassis imported from de Dion in France. But trolley men felt that this was clearly a freak of local circumstance. Fifth Avenue was snobbishly hostile to streetcars, just as all of Manhattan (like Washington, D.C.) was stubbornly hostile to overhead wires, forcing the use of high-cost and troublesome conduit systems. Fifth Avenue's buses might be locally successful—there were thirty-five of the things running by 1908—but they signified little. Any respectable car line could have carried more people in its trolleys, and probably faster and cheaper too. In 1912 a Cleveland street railway tried out a few gasoline-driven buses and found that they did indeed have a minor utility, as outlying feeders for established trolley lines.

It was also true, streetcar men knew, that an absurd vehicle called a "trackless trolley" or "trolley omnibus" was periodically being invented. This was more sensible in that it drew energy from a central power plant, but there appeared to be little else of serious merit to it. Siemens & Halske had uncorked one of the things in Berlin in 1899; another had briefly turned up in Scranton in 1903; and still other incarnations had short trials in California and Wisconsin in 1912 and 1913. No matter: they signified only that some people failed to understand the enormous strength and value of the existing trolley car.

Then, in the summer of 1914, something happened that even the most complacent streetcar superintendent couldn't ignore. Within six months it flared up into a portent that for trolley cars was as urgent and perilous as a firebell in the night. In the manner of portents, it seemed obscure and meaningless at first. On about July 1 of that year, a private automobile pulled up at streetcar stops in Los Angeles and its driver informed the persons waiting there that he would be pleased to offer rides down the avenue at a "jitney"—a nickel—a head. This was the first tiny

Soon fender-flapping flivvers nosed up to the car stops, and the Model T revolution had begun.

beginning of disaster.

The early jitney was a remarkable phenomenon, in some ways akin to such historical curiosities as the chain-letter and midget-golf crazes. By the late summer of 1914, word-of-mouth tales spread across the land of staggering profits earned by private-car owners who went jitneying. It was whispered that a man could clear enough in a month to pay for his car, and enough in a year or two to retire in comfort. The stories won wide credence. Soon fender-flapping flivvers and shabby old limousines were nosing up to the car stops to try their luck at the new gold strike. A car owner with a job might hunt up an unemployed man to go shares with him as a driver, or he might try jitneying himself after work in the evening rush hour. People who had been searching for an excuse to buy their first car seized on the jitney idea as justification. Many a man irked by his foreman or the size of his pay envelope quit his job, blew his savings on a secondhand flivver, and gave the notion a whirl.

Jitneys spread with astonishing speed. Six months after the first one appeared in Los Angeles, 700 were estimated to be cruising the streets of that city alone. Soon they were also skimming the cream from high-traffic lines in Middle Western and Eastern cities. For reasons now obscure, they caught on particularly hard in some areas; New Jersey for example was a jitney hotbed by 1916. Part of the explanation for their national growth was that they were a fad, but there were other factors. Streetcars *were* slow and extremely uncomfortable in the rush hour, when they inched along in a torpid fashion appropriate to a utility without competition. Trolleys were dull, too;

they'd been around *forever*. For many people in 1914, an automobile ride was an exciting novelty. In a jitney you could have this experience for a nickel, and instead of dangling from a strap in a crowded, surly atmosphere, you could sit down on upholstered leather and chat companionably with your driver and fellow riders.

This was the first time in the quarter-century history of trolley cars that a sharp prick of outside competition was felt. The immediate response was a loud howl of outrage. Jitneys, it was repeatedly proclaimed, were irregular and irresponsible. They kept no schedules, met no standards, and provided no service in off hours or to outlying districts. Instead they clustered parasitically around a few heavy-traffic lines during the rush hour, stealing fares from the solid, respectable trolleys that provided the finest mass transportation in the world. They dumped their riders after as short a trip as could be contrived and darted back to steal more fares. They jockeyed about in an erratic and dangerous way. Often they were uninsured and they represented so little net worth that a rider injured in an accident had no source from which to recover damages. They were a violation of the spirit, if not the letter, of franchise agreements. Worst of all, they were *unfair*, because they totally evaded the heavy tax burdens borne by franchised trolleys.

There was of course a broad strain of justice in these howls. Jitneys achieved legal status by a kind of default; the automobile was unknown when most city codes and state laws were shaped. Streetcar companies sent their lawyers trotting to the transit commissions, legislatures, and courts. Unremitting political pressure and legal action in a few years closed the gaps through which the jitney had emerged. Here and there a few jitneys survived, pushed in the direction of corporate respectability, and transmuted into small bus lines that soon began to use specially-built bodies on motor-truck chassis. But not many jitney drivers banded together to fight back; hacking at a nickel a head turned out to be something less than the Comstock Lode.

By 1919 trolleys in the United States were clearly emerging victorious from their first competitive brush. It could hardly have been otherwise in such an uneven contest between a few thousand flivvers and an industry that, in 1917, had 44,800 miles of track, employed 295,000 people, and toted passengers at the rate of 11.3 billion annually. What was most signifi-

cant, perhaps, about the jitney flurry was the way in which streetcar companies had instinctively responded with legal weapons. The trolley had grown to be a utility of giant proportions, but its troubles, growing larger by the day, were not even remotely the kind that could be averted by sending lawyers to weave webs around impertinent competitors.

Up until the twenties, the stubbornest trolley problem seemed to be operating expenses, which climbed like a sick man's fever. Even before the war the operating ratio—the relationship between revenue and expense—had begun to show an alarming turn for the worse. Each year all of the thousands of materials and services needed to run a trolley line cost more: copper and steel, powerhouse coal and the

On a Sunday afternoon in the spring of 1921, autos were crowding streetcars near Van Cortlandt Park in New York City.

This long trolley, an unsuccessful experiment in cutting labor costs, was spliced together from two St. Louis cars.

printing of transfers, sand for slippery rails and the wage scales needed to keep employees from flocking to better jobs in factories and shipyards. The rising passenger totals added bright spots of color to the patient's cheeks, but with operating expense rising uncontrollably, the outlook was not cheering.

There were other headaches. Passenger discontent with slow schedules and crowding was swelling slowly, building up pressure that couldn't be laughed off indefinitely. Maintenance was another slow-burning fuse. With operating expense under severe scrutiny, the natural place to pare a bit to keep the dividends coming was maintenance, even though this was a measure that simply banked future difficulties at compound interest. Wartime scarcities helped justify postponing repairs, but few things decay more decisively than a poorly maintained streetcar system—on trolleys, a scabrous squalor lurks close below the surface, and track in particular can get hopelessly decrepit

without proper attention. Finally, labor shortages were exceedingly troublesome in many areas. To the frank horror of old hands, a few lines had to experiment with hiring conductorettes and motorladies.

In the fall of 1916, as the first high tide of these troubles began to swirl around company managers, an exciting new car appeared that promised for a time to make everything right again. This was the Birney Safety Car, a lightweight, one-man car that was especially created as medicine for the industry's ills. It was an immediate hit and hundreds of Birney cars were soon on order. (Students of business history may be struck by the fact that the streetcar industry, born of Sprague's brilliant ideas, has repeatedly found solace in the dream that all its difficulties might be dispelled by some wonderful new design.)

Charles O. Birney was an engineer for Stone & Webster, a company that operated many streetcar systems. He had earlier helped design a "standard car" along conventional lines, which lent itself to manufacturing economies. But his 1916 car was something different: a calculated return to the single-truck vehicle of earlier days. It had a rounded roof that was both strong and cheap to build, as well as a stressed-skin body, engineered in what would later be thought of as the aircraft tradition. It weighed 13,000 pounds, compared to the 30,000 to 40,000 pounds of its predecessors, and its two 25-horsepower motors supplied perky acceleration. It was a two-door double-ender, intended from the start for one-man operation. A few one-man cars had been tried before by impoverished lines, but they had never been acceptable on big-city systems, where it was feared that the public would think them dangerous. Birney cars—the word Safety was at first always coupled to the name—had such built-in precautions as an interlock to keep the car from moving when a door was open and a dead-man's controller that stopped the car if the motorman-conductor (now evasively called the "operator") toppled over in a fit. Though the public turned out not to care much one way or the other about safety aspects of one-man operation, the trolley companies were highly delighted at the prospects of both licking the labor shortage and trimming the labor cost per car.

Thousands of Birneys were purchased in the years between 1916 and 1921. Their virtues included more than just paring labor costs. They were easier on the track; they consumed less electricity; and they were capable of higher schedule speeds than any previous cars. This meant that a company could afford to schedule more frequent service, something that, according to efficiency experts, was basic in preventing rider discontent. The doctrine was enunciated in the slogan "A car in sight at all times."

After 1921 the Birneys fell from favor almost as fast as they came up. It grew obvious that the cars really weren't large enough to cope with heavy rush-hour traffic on big-city lines, and this was a serious flaw. Nor were they particularly good as snow fighters. (Commented one operator morosely: "In two inches of snow, a Birney might not move at all. Just sit there and hum like hell.") On some suburban lines they also won a reputation for derailing easily, though this may have been unfair, since many a small suburban line had fallen so far behind on track maintenance that almost any car might have careened off the rails. The riding public, which had never felt

The first pilot-model Birney Safety Car was built in 1916.

Often trolley poles on Birneys sprouted from built-up roof stands; the poles would otherwise have had to be too long.

Following in the wake of a heavy interurban, a Birney rolls down a flivver-lined street in Sheboygan, Wis., in 1922.

Coupled in a train, four San Diego trolleys tear along.

the same passionate enthusiasm for Birneys that management did, fell into the habit of deriding the cars as Dinkys and Galloping Gerties. In college towns it was observed that a few young men could, by rhythmical jouncing, cause a Birney to wallow like a foundering barque, and that with skill and application, the poor thing could sometimes be bounced clean off the rails.

Although the little cars lost their popularity, they left a permanent mark. On most lines they were replaced by what has been generally called "double-truck Birneys"—bigger cars that changed to the greater capacity of double trucks, but that retained one-man operation and comparatively light weight. The original Birneys are not absolutely dead yet; a few are still reported to be cavorting along in smaller South American and Far Eastern cities. Given the juice, they'll run till they fall apart.

So many companies were in receivership during and immediately after the First World War that

By the mid-twenties, buses began to spread. Cleveland, 1925.

President Wilson appointed a Federal Electric Railway Commission to investigate and recommend. In due course, after collecting thousands of pages of testimony, the commission reported that trolleys had indeed a great many troubles. Apart from automobiles, three of the principal ones identified were (1) public and political unwillingness to accept increase of the time-honored five-cent fare; (2) complex franchise structures in which "underliers"—holders of ancient but still valid permissive rights—were too heavy a financial drain; and (3) excessive special tax burdens, such as paving and bridge-maintenance assessments. The commission may have helped; at least in cities where taxes were eased, franchises tidied up, and fare increases or zone-fare systems permitted, companies did better.

Still it was painfully clear during the twenties that trolleys were coasting downhill fast. Company securities, far from being the comfort of widows and the favorite of high-collared trustees, had become cats

Streetcars grew to be irrelevant in residential suburbs.

Before the end, interurban cars grew magnificently in pomp and presence. This one posed regally in 1930 at Delaware, Ohio.

and dogs. The mileage of electrified track had hit its peak back in 1918 and had steadily dwindled each year since. (Plenty of new track was laid after then, of course, but never enough to make up for the increasing abandonments.) Somewhat like a moribund whale, the trolley industry was so large that it kept growing even after it had begun to die. Passenger riding kept inching slowly upward until 1923, when the total hit 14 billion rides annually. Then riding too began to slope steeply downward.

Buses were still rare at the beginning of the decade. In the whole country less than seventy-five buses were operated by street railways in 1920. But as tidings spread that buses could cut losses and even actually earn money, they came on in a thundering stampede. Typically the pattern was for buses to be used first out along the fringes of the system, where it was obviously cheaper to use them than to extend the rail and wire. Later, as operating-expense figures became more eloquent, buses took over trolley branches that had moderate traffic but high costs. The last stronghold of the streetcar, and the place where it consistently did best, was the heavily traveled main line.

But pure cost accounting was only part of the competition between trolley and bus. What trolley partisans described acrimoniously as "bustitution" was often decided on grounds other than cost-per-mile. If a city council stubbornly refused to budge an inch on an onerous paving assessment, it was natural to counter by abandoning the track. Where the rail or overhead had grown so dilapidated as to need heavy capital expenditure, it was natural to spend the money on buses instead. Where changing neighborhoods and new directions of city growth had left an old trolley line high and dry, it was natural to use a more flexible bus line to hunt out the relocated traffic. Many a streetcar superintendent, surveying the havoc that the years were bringing, put it all down to the mystical theory that "everybody wants to ride on rubber."

It was more than that, of course, though trolley men can scarcely be blamed for not knowing. Even a quarter century later the full implication of the automobile cannot be wholly fathomed. Growing quite rationally from a rich man's toy to transportation for an ordinary man, it suddenly exploded in the

Encountering an interurban train as it wended along a city street could both startle and frustrate an impatient driver.

twenties and later into a hundred other things as well. It became a widely employed means of expressing caste, a method of subduing yearnings for escape and power, and a device that both stimulated and sated the national taste for mobility. It afforded, further, opportunities for the display of skill and the ventilation of personality. Because it had all these possibilities and filled all these needs, it has grown into an immense part of the nation's economic structure. It has reshaped customs, changed both city and country, killed a score of industries, and spawned a hundred others. Dowdy old streetcars had about as much chance against the auto as mule cars would have.

While much of this was mercifully obscure in the twenties, men who'd spent their life with trolleys could see by 1925 that the country was deep in the new gasoline era. In the old days, for example, a real-estate development would be planned with a view to its trolley service; but now streetcars were irrelevant in residential suburbs. (In many neighborhoods it even became a disadvantage to be on a trolley line.) Once the gaiety and lights of Electric Park had magically attracted family groups and courting couples; now the independence and freedom conferred by the family car made trolley riding seem entirely different, utilitarian and a little grubby. The idea of a trolley-tour vacation somehow became grotesque. Certainly trolley-riding was no longer thought of as fun, as a verse in the Sante Fe Railroad magazine pointed out:

Any girl can be gay in a classy coupé;
In a taxicab all can be jolly.
But the girl worth the while is the one who can smile
When you're taking her home on the trolley!

Not every shaky streetcar system contrived a gradual conversion to buses. With a Götterdämmerung touch, some lines were terminated by fire. From the beginning carbarns had been highly combustible, perhaps because of the conjunction of oil-soaked floors, wooden roof beams, and infinite possibilities for electrical or kerosene-lantern mischance. But where in the great days a severe carbarn fire meant little more than borrowing rolling stock from another company until new cars could be delivered, now it was likely to be the final catastrophe.

Disastrous fires happened most often late at night, when the barn was banked with sleeping cars. The night man would catch a whiff of smoke and begin frenzied efforts to get the power on and raise trolley poles so that the cars could be run outside. But old cars were quite as combustible as their barns, and often the outcome was a flaming funeral for the line's rolling stock and an end to its dreary, receiver-ridden

Carbarns were always remarkably combustible. Quebec, 1921.

existence. Typical of scores of similar fires was the following one, described for *Railroad Magazine* by Stephen D. Maguire:

Sixteen out of a total of nineteen cars in the barn of the Mauch Chunk & Leighton Transit Company were destroyed by a fire during the last years of that line's existence when the Mauch Chunk barn burned on December 29, 1923. At 3 A.M. on the morning of the fire the night man was working in a pit under a car in the old frame car house and shop. He heard a strange crackling noise and upon crawling from beneath the car, saw flames coming from the west end of the barn where the shop was located.

He ran to the powerhouse and sent in an alarm, then went back to the barn and tried to fight the fire with a small extinguisher—to no effect. The powerhouse attendant started up the generators to pull the cars out of the burning building. A line car and two closed cars, 31 and 32, were removed, the last car catching fire as it came out of the barn. The wires came down behind this car, preventing any further removals. The barn was almost a complete wreck by the time the Mauch Chunk Volunteer Department arrived, and all they could do was to prevent the spread of the fire to nearby buildings.

Very often a similar end came to other surviving monuments of the great days when big open cars rollicked out to Electric Park by the lake or sea. The old wooden dance halls and pavilions, boarded up for the season, would catch fire some windy winter night, lighting up the sky for an hour or so before they, too, were gone.

In some respects an interurban was more vulnerable to the gasoline engine than was a city streetcar. A large city *had* to have some form of mass transportation, however unprofitable, if it was not to choke to death. But the interurbans had staked their future on providing moderate-distance intercity transportation, something that the gasoline engine could supply exceedingly well. Private cars soaked up a big share of passenger traffic, and intercity buses (rolling on the constantly improving roads that the auto was bringing) took away some of the rest. Freight business was steadily lost to trucks, which could compete by offering door-to-door service, and which required less freight-handling steps.

The short, sharp depression of 1921 had brought abandonment to some of the shakier interurban lines. It also raised serious questions about the future of the industry, even though, during the twenties, most of the interurban network of the United States remained intact. Some companies resolved to combat their troubles by such classic means as improved service and a determined hunt for new business. Schedules were speeded up; fast and luxurious new cars were ordered; delivery systems set up for freight; and budgets for advertising and promotion increased.

Sometimes the promotion became a bit fanciful, as when the Pacific Electric offered its regular riders academic courses to be studied en route, with credits awarded for successful completion. While this idea can hardly have generated much traffic, the picture of a carful of commuters swotting away at geometric theorems or irregular French verbs is an arresting

As extinction neared, many big cars grew shabby and lonely, like these last few passenger cars on the Fort Dodge line.

Tearing past a highway crossing at 60 miles an hour, its air horn echoing, an Indiana Railroad car raced to Terre Haute.

one. On other lines traffic promotion took the form of a theatrical stunt, as when the Cincinnati & Lake Erie staged a race between an interurban and an airplane. Newsreel cameras showed theater audiences all over the country a big electric cleanly defeating a Jenny biplane, at least on one straight rural stretch; where the plane was when the car was moseying through city traffic wasn't discussed.

Showmanship and better service weren't enough. When the depression struck in 1929, virtually the whole interurban industry collapsed with dismaying speed. No interurbans survived in New England after 1933, and the big cars disappeared from New York and much of the East soon after. In the Middle West, where they had been most strongly entrenched, they fared only a little less badly. Two large consolidations (the Indiana Railroad and the Cincinnati & Lake Erie) were patched together from a number of sick lines, but they too gave way in a few years. For many a company, revenues sank below actual operating costs, without a penny left for maintenance and repair, fixed expense, and the rest of the bookkeeping columns. As the thirties ran out, the great complex of interurbans in Ohio, Indiana, and Michigan vanished.

A few hardy lines survived, in Iowa, Illinois, and California. Some even picked up a bit under the special conditions prevailing during World War II, when gasoline and rubber were precious and when any-

For the benefit of Pathé newsreel cameras, Cincinnati & Lake Erie's No. 126 outdistanced a biplane near Dayton in 1930.

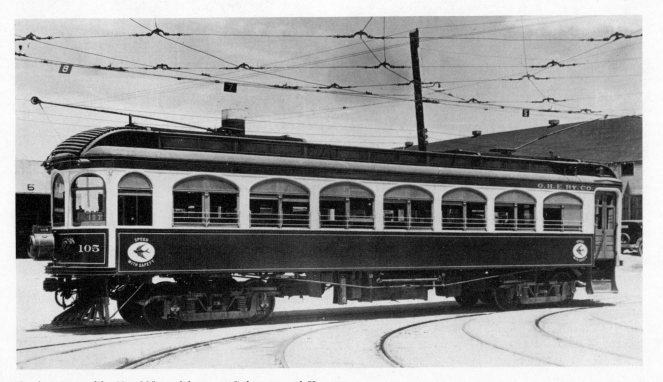

Handsome cars like No. 105 sped between Galveston and Houston.

thing on rails could find work to do. But the relentless pressures came back again after the war. Only a handful of lines survive today, their futures depending on concentrated commuting traffic or highway congestion. In all but motive power, they closely resemble railroads.

When the interurban companies were being decimated, and the big pompous cars were committed to the cutting torch, twinges of sadness were felt by all who remembered the great days. Sometimes the recollection had a tartly ironic sting, as at Indianapolis.

Here the large Traction Terminal—which had once echoed to the arrival and departure of hundreds of interurbans each day—now echoed still, but to the blatting exhausts of buses.

The air of irreproachable dignity often remained to the end.

11. RUST IN PEACE

But oh! may there never come the day,
  Be it ever yet so far,
When a child shall go to his dad and say,
As a youngster might, in his curious way,
  What was a trolley car?

—*From a 35-stanza ballad by Robert S. Wilson,*
a trolley fan of Yakima, Washington

As the disastrous decade of the twenties ended, a large number of streetcar lines were in sad shape, in physical equipment as well as in finances. Years of pared-down maintenance had seriously hurt the track and wiring. Tens of thousands of cars were growing raffish or dilapidated. With cars, though, the situation was paradoxical: trolleys, being traditionally "over-built" to begin with, never seemed to wear out fast enough for their companies' best interests. They had, instead, a kind of aggravated durability. By 1929 many a car was grinding and squealing along

after thirty years of service—almost four times as long as a bus was expected to last. Weary old cars that had clocked 40,000 or 50,000 miles a year for three decades were commonplace. Though this durability was often viewed with pride by streetcar men, it exacted its penalties in torpid performance, obsolescence of design and materials, and a tendency to depress the customers.

Beginning in 1929, the streetcar industry tackled the problem in an impressive piece of collective action. Twenty-five of the larger companies banded to-

GOOD-BYE, MY FRIENDS, GOOD-BYE.

GOOD-BYE MY FRIENDS, THIS IS THE END; I'VE TRAVELLED MILES AND MILES, AND WATCHED YOUR FACES THROUGH THE YEARS, SHOW ANGER, TEARS AND SMILES ALTHOUGH YOU'VE CRITICIZED MY LOOKS — AND SAID I WAS TOO SLOW, I GOT YOU THERE AND BROUGHT YOU BACK, THROUGH RAIN AND SLEET AND SNOW.

This lugubrious and whiskered Birney made its final trip in Halifax, Nova Scotia, in 1949. Seven years earlier the streetcars of that city had carried some 32 million people annually.

Over Brooklyn Bridge new PCCs glided in unnatural silence.

gether in a group called the "Electric Railway Presidents' Conference Committee." The PCC pooled its ideas on what an ideal trolley should be like. It collected more than a million dollars from the entire industry for a research staff. It hired as its chief engineer a man without prior experience in trolley-car design, on the theory that this was one way to avoid perpetuating untested past assumptions. Research was begun in such basic areas as how fast a car could be started without agitating the straphangers excessively. (The rate turned out to be high—as much as 4.5 m.p.h. per second, provided it was smooth.) After nearly five years of work, the PCC group unveiled their "dream streetcar," which is the streamliner that is chiefly running today. To the wonderment of all, it glided along on its trial runs in spooky silence, with none of the abrasive growling that trolleys had emitted for nearly fifty years. Other virtues included smooth but brisk acceleration, powerful brakes, a quiet ride, and such automobile gadgetry as pedal controls, sealed-beam headlights, and a pair of bright red stoplights on its rump. First shown at a trolley-officials' convention in 1934, a PCC car gave a trial ride to Frank Sprague, just a few weeks before the old gentleman died.

PCC cars were in widespread use by the late thirties and they proved to be capable performers. "Operators" (i.e., motormen), company treasurers, and the riding public all liked them. About the only dissident voices raised were those of confirmed trolley enthusiasts. These fans, a nostalgic lot, came to regard the PCC car with chilly respect mixed with distaste. For them a PCC car ran much too well; it had no *character;* and it looked rather like a bus, a kind of ultimate depravity.

For all its slick tricks, the PCC car has managed more to delay than to avert the steady abandonment of streetcar trackage. It seems possible, as some trolley partisans argue, that if PCCs had arrived on the scene sooner, the lumbering, oily-breathed buses might not have had so easy a series of triumphs. And it is demonstrable that in certain special circumstances—notably, high-density runs on wide streets—trolleys are *still* superior to buses at carrying the most people at the highest speed for the least cost. The point, though, is becoming increasingly academic. In recent years, total riding on all city transit has dwindled steadily; and whenever there is a trolley-vs.-bus issue in a city, the arguments take on a predictable pattern. For trolleys there is a bit of sentimental partisanship (doubtless weakened a little by the denatured personality of PCC cars) and a mention of the special cases in which a trolley can shine.

In behalf of buses there is no sentimental advocacy whatever (it is difficult to love a bus) but simply a listing of competitive advantages. These usually include lower costs, the safety and convenience of curb loading, freedom from blockages, flexibility of routing, somewhat less hostility from motorists and truckers, and the broadly popular elimination of rails and overhead wires. These are, in total, difficult arguments for trolley partisans to counter.

Once the bus battle has been fought and lost in a community, other developments also become predictable. Trolley fans talk with deep loathing about the pernicious spread of "bustitution." Newspapers do a Sunday feature on how the trolley is joining the bobtail horsecar in a Valhalla of bygone vehicles. Company lawyers fence with city authorities over who's to pay the coming cost of repaving the streets after the tracks come out. An old-time motorman is assigned to a rite known as the Last Run, which is attended by a body of trolley fans and, sometimes, by a few drunks attracted by the odor of souvenirs. As the Last Run approaches the carbarn its riders energetically remove such mementoes as roll signs, control handles, fare registers, gongs, and anything else that can be loosened with pocket tools.

The New Year's Eve flavor to a last run has not always been present. Richard H. Steinmetz once wrote an account of the final trip of a beloved Penn-

The first PCC car to run in Brooklyn, as photographed in 1936.

Just before the riot started. A last run in Norfolk, Va., ended with broken windows, disabled car, and the cops called out.

sylvania interurban that has become a classic among fans:

It was 11:30 P.M. of a moonlight night in June that Harry Sperrow, motorman of the first trolley, wrote finis to a long chapter in his life. Valley Railways No. 2, a venerable Jackson & Sharp car, was to make the final return trip to Carlisle. . . . We stood in a little knot on the station platform. The rotary converter inside hummed a weird little song of farewell as the operator shook hands with Harry. With a deep sigh from her air brakes, No. 2 moved slowly off into the moondrenched countryside on the last trip.

Somehow none of us on the front platform felt much like talking until Locust Point, where the line left the highway. Then it was as if the pent-up waters of a dam were released. Everybody recalled incidents that were amusing or sad. Before we knew it we were at Churchtown. A few streetlights were burning, revealing the lone figure of a man opposite the general store and post office. He proved to be the last and only passenger to Carlisle. Harvey Clay, our conductor, took his fare, rang it up, and then sat down to talk with him while we left Churchtown to its slumbers. . . .

A soft night breeze filled the car with sweet-smelling

Last car in a Maryland county.

country air. Every hill, curve, and tangent on the weed-grown right-of-way brought back more memories. The cemetery where Harry and another old-timer had the scare of their lives one dark night. Near Lutztown was the place where the snow-sweeper and two other cars were snowbound for two days back in 1918. Boiling Springs and the trolley park there, and the gay picnics of yesteryear that had required every available car on the system. The ancient hostelry where an all-night celebration had marked the arrival of the first car in 1898. . . .

Old No. 2 was clicking off the miles, drawing nearer and nearer to the end of a familiar existence. Then there was Hogan's Alley on the outskirts of Carlisle, and the old carbarn. Harry said it wouldn't be proper to quit right there. We rolled past the barn into town. It was now 12:45 and the town slept a deep sleep. The tree-lined streets were deserted, and when we stopped in Carlisle Square there wasn't a soul in sight—only marble Molly Pitcher and her cannon. There was a lump in my throat as I changed poles for Harry and swung up onto the back platform to ring the bell for the last time. In a few blocks we were back at the barn. No. 2's lights went out as the trolley pole was hooked down, and then she was swallowed up in darkness as the barn lights were extinguished.

Once the Last Run is done, the trolley company must face up to a considerable disposal problem. There's the overhead (copper is money in the bank) and the steel rails (fine scrap but not always easy to mine from the pavement). There's also a score or two of old streetcars that, each being maybe 45 feet long and weighing 30 tons, can't simply be stuffed in the corporate attic. So off the old cars go to the scrap yard, for fiery dissection by cutting torch and future reincarnation as freshly poured metal. Sometimes whole fleets of cars can be sold intact to foreign cities not so infatuated with buses; many an old trolley from the United States is still clanging its gong in Latin America. And sometimes scrapping stops short with the trucks and machinery, the car bodies being translated to a new, stationary life as hamburger stands, beach cottages, clubhouses, hen coops, tool sheds, and, in one recorded instance in Mississippi, a church.

During the abandonment of a Cleveland line not long ago, the old affinity of trolleys for the offbeat mischance turned up once more, faint but unmistakable. Miles of rail had been uprooted and most of

Awaiting reincarnation, Pacific Electric cars here were cut in manageable pieces and then fed into open-hearth furnaces.

End of the line, at Queens, N.Y., for two sturdy old trolleys.

Trolley poles writhing in the flames, seven old cars undergo scrap-yard cremation. The preliminary burning is simply to aid later steps of cutting up and segregating the scrap metals.

The last man aboard this Lehigh Valley streetcar—a modern Allentown, Pa., car—pictured while lying on its side at a Beth-lehem plant. Next step: burn everything burnable.

Stripped old trolleys, pictured in 1939 at New Bern, N.C.

the overhead cut down before someone discovered a solitary 35-ton trolley marooned at the far end of the line. It took the services of a huge flatbed trailer, with a flush of corporate embarrassment, to bring the forlorn old thing home to be scrapped.

Streetcars have always had admirers, men who simply felt a liking for the cars or for the pleasant associations that they brought back. But only in comparatively recent years have trolley enthusiasts banded into societies formed to celebrate the glory of a vanishing vehicle. The streetcar fan—there are presently about 4,000 of them in the country—is a paradoxical fellow. His deepest motivations are clearly bound up with sentiment, and yet he often develops some sharply focused specialty that helps him conceal this. He is a collector of transfers, or an expert on the arc headlights in use in 1910, or an authority on the complete roster of cars on a long-defunct line. It is no trick at all, however, to discern that beneath his *expertise* ("The only Jewett that ever ran on the C G & P was No. 362, and she split a switch near Illyria in May, 1913, and was junked.") there is a deeper current of recollection. Perhaps it was the time

Its rolling days done, this elderly interurban at least has a sedentary, window-curtained life in a field of wildflowers.

The day in 1939 that buses took over a Gary interurban, fans chartered this car. Here one man thumbs his nose at the bus.

Loyal streetcar fans, riding a special car near Wilkes-Barre in 1940, pushed it back under a live wire when it ran onto a dead section of the overhead. A slight downgrade helped out.

as a youngster when he first rode an interurban to the city; or the excitement of getting a job at twenty as a *real* motorman on the extra list. Or it may be memory of a courtship facilitated by excursions to Electric Park, and of a young lady willing to have her risibles tickled by witty reference to an interurban as an "Uncle Reuben." Whatever the half-remembered roots of his attitudes, he's a man with a genuine fondness for the old cars, and an implacable hatred of buses.

He can even find cause, in these dark days, for a flickering flame of hope. After all, he argues, the last trolley hasn't made its last run yet. In many parts of the world—including much of Europe, Russia, Japan, and Latin America—the electric car is very far from dead. Even on this continent, some streetcars are going to be running for a long time still.

Fleets of cars still operate in Boston, Newark, Philadelphia, Pittsburgh, Cleveland, Toronto, El Paso, and San Francisco. There is a distinct chance, the trolley enthusiast feels, that there will be a metamorphosis of the cars into some healthy future institution. Perhaps it will be a trolley-and-interurban hybrid, like Cleveland's Shaker Heights Rapid Transit. Perhaps it will be a surface-and-subway system, with cars running above ground in uptown areas and in subways in the desperately congested downtown districts, as is presently working successfully in Boston and Newark. Whatever pattern the future takes, the loyal fan feels that electric cars are *much* too fine not to survive.

The concentrated interest of trolley enthusiasts is remarkable. Before track abandonments became so general, many a man made a point of riding on every

Recent acquisitions at the Seashore museum in Maine: a Dallas city car, a double-decker from England, a Montreal interurban.

line within hundreds of miles of his home, just so he could see what each was like. Others have published pamphlets detailing the complete history of favorite lines, right down to the number assigned to each car that the company ever owned, and what it was changed to in any subsequent renumbering. Others have concentrated on amassing data about motors or brakes, timetables or fare registers. Collecting pictures of trolleys is a favorite hobby; and during the war years fans were occasionally picked up by the police, having been turned in by suspicious patriots who had seen them photographing carbarns and rolling stock. William James Sidis (an extraordinary person who had first won notice as a child prodigy, graduating magna cum laude from Harvard at fifteen) once published an impressive tome on peridromophily—a term he coined for the hobby of collecting streetcar transfers. Writing under the pseudonym of Frank Folupa, Sidis prescribed in minute detail how such a collection should be organized and displayed. His approach was one of intense solemnity:

There may be some interest in expressing in verse form (for easier memorizing) information concerning routing and transfer privileges. . . . [For example,] the following is a verse we made up on the opening of the Cambridge Subway (Boston-Cambridge, March 23, 1912):

A Seashore treasure is this fast "Crandic" interurban. Its name derives from the Cedar Rapids and Iowa City Railway.

Another prize is this Los Angeles car with its curved windows.

The Cambridge Subway's open now;
The subway trains are heard.
'Twas in the year of nineteen twelve,
On March the twenty-third.

Perhaps the earliest large trolley-enthusiast society to be organized was the Electric Railroaders' Association. It was founded in 1934 by an energetic and talented engineer named E. J. Quinby, who had been a motorman for a time in his youth. The E.R.A. has about 2,000 members, mainly in the Northeast though some with "divisions" in other parts of the country. It publishes a monthly magazine called *ERA Headlights* and also occasionally issues special pamphlets on an individual line or topic. One E.R.A. activity—in common with most other groups in the field—is running occasional outings called "fan trips." These are tours, often on chartered cars, of some surviving "juice system," and they are convivial junkets marked by snapping and swapping pictures, making tape recordings and movies of trolleys in action, and happily exchanging specialized information. In the Middle West a somewhat smaller but highly active organization is a Chicago group called the Central Electric Railfans Association. The C.E.R.A.

puts out a lavish and remarkably detailed annual history of some aspects of past electric-car glory. On the national scene, E.R.A.'s principal competitor is a more formal body called the National Railway Historical Society. The N.R.H.S. was formed in 1935 by some Pennsylvania enthusiasts, and it concerns itself with both steam and electric lines. It has a membership of almost 2,000 persons in about sixteen local chapters, holds an annual convention to which hundreds of faithful fans journey, and has a tradition of putting out lovingly prepared historical papers.

By far the most ambitious task that trolley enthusiasts have tackled has been the establishment of trolley museums—havens where old cars would be safe from the cutting torch and where they could be lovingly restored to their original condition and maybe even run a little on a stretch of private track. Conventional museums have not of course entirely neglected the streetcar; institutions like the Museum of the City of New York and the Henry Ford Museum in Dearborn have embalmed a very few old cars in a kind of varnished and steam-heated amber. But this is not at all what the trolley enthusiast has

Festooned with students, No. 840 makes its last Yale Bowl run.

Moldering in the woods, No. 840 faces only corruption and rot.

Lovingly restored, No. 840 has a new life at Warehouse Point.

in mind. To him there are so many fine old cars on the verge of disappearing, and they have so many evocative excitements, that his dream of a proper museum is entirely different. He envisions a working, outdoor street railway, stocked with cars that he has helped rescue and restore, that will both preserve a bit of the cherished past and supply opportunities for playing trains in an acceptably adult fashion.

In the summer of 1939 a handful of Bostonians, on a last run of the Biddeford & Saco line in Maine, were grieving at the thought that the fine old twelve-bench open car which they were riding was doomed to be junked. In the manner of New Englanders, they promptly formed a society to Do Something About It. They bought the trolley and had it trucked to a pasture outside Kennebunkport, Maine. By the time

The old roofs must be made weathertight at trolley museums.

En route to Warehouse Point, an elderly open car rides on rubber through Hartford. The truck, owned by Seashore, was lent to its sister trolley-car museum for the transportation job.

of Pearl Harbor they had incorporated with a re-sounding name (New England Electric Railway Historical Society) and had brought four old cars to sanctuary in the pasture. In the next fifteen years the pasture—now christened the Seashore Electric Railway—had a phenomenal development. There are presently about forty-five cars, rescued from fourteen states and abroad. Many of them have been lovingly restored and most of them are at least protected from further deterioration. There is half a mile of track, a powerhouse, a carbarn, and an ambitious program of expansion. There are about three hundred active members, including a nucleus of twenty-five or thirty persons having a demonstrated willingness to work to the verge of exhaustion for the sake of the idea.

Seashore's example inspired similar enterprises in other parts of the country. By 1955 there were some fifteen other groups in the United States and Canada at work in preserving about 160 streetcars, ranging all the way from ancient bobtails to the light-alloy "high-speeds" that a few interurban lines resorted to in their final years of extremity. So enthusiastically has the museum idea taken hold that the day is not far off, as some fans have wryly computed, when there will be more trolley museums than working trolley companies.

Besides Seashore, two other collections are thriving in New England. One, near Warehouse Point, Connecticut, has a dozen-odd old cars, 1,200 feet of electrified track, and fine plans for its three-mile right-of-way. The other, near Branford, Connecticut, rivals Seashore in the size of its collection, and leads all other museums in regularly operating a few cars on weekends for the enjoyment of its members and anyone else who happens to drop in. (With luck and tact, a mannerly visitor may even get to be a motorman himself for a short run, and a thoroughly enjoyable experience it is.) Branford has almost a mile of track, thirty-three cars, several steel carbarns, and a Diesel-powered generator that produces ample current to tickle the old motors into motion. The museum is the product of labors by its membership so arduous that it is exhausting just to think about them.

Elsewhere in the country are a number of other museums, most of them not as far developed, though there is a working collection with six cars and two-thirds of a mile of track at Worthington, Ohio. In many cities the development has progressed only to the storage of one or two old cars as a core for the collection, and to the slow hunt for money, land, and a nucleus of hardworking devotees. The job of creating a trolley museum is decidedly difficult, far more

so than it seems in the first fine flush of incorporation. There is generally very little money to spend, and the work itself must usually be contributed in weekend driblets, weather and wives permitting. In the field of antique collecting there are few *objets* as monumentally cumbersome as a trolley car, which may weigh several dozen tons and which may have to be transported, not under its own power, several hun-

A graceful, winding stretch along the Branford right-of-way.

dred miles to sanctuary. Once there, it needs protection from small boys with slingshots and other casual vandals that like to shoot at windows, and from the weather, which can penetrate an aging roof to spread a dismaying blight of rot and rust.

Everything about restoring a trolley is laborious and outsize, though true fans know it's worth it. Refinishing may take hundreds of hours of work. Repairing and renewing intricate old control and brake systems takes patience and a special feeling for by-gone mechanisms. Laying track and switches, erecting poles, and stringing overhead is physically a tough job. Finding some kind of power supply that will feed 500 volts of direct current to elderly trolley motors can be a major stumbling block, for direct current is virtually unobtainable from ordinary power lines, and some worn-out Diesel-driven generator may have to be rebuilt. The harried, first-things-first aspect of running a trolley museum often gives the place the look (especially to wives) of an oddly spe-

Pride and joy of the Branford museum, this Diesel generates the current needed to tickle ancient motors and compressors to life. It also required long months of patient rebuilding.

cialized dump; but to the true streetcar enthusiast it is a kind of Elysian field, worth every drop of the perspiration it took.

As trolleys come closer each year to commercial extinction, the work that these enthusiasts have performed grows steadily more valuable. For though the memory of streetcars will remain green for a generation or two yet, it is dismaying to discover how recollection can soften and round into a generalized blur, until all that remains is a memory of a memory. But if at one of these museums you climb aboard some familiar old trolley, you'll be astonished to find yourself sliding back three or four decades in time. You'll sniff that long-forgotten but familiar odor compounded of paint, hot motors, and track sand. You'll feel the same ponderous lurch as the rails steer the old car on its course. You'll hear the rattle of the windows, the detuned *clonk* of the gong, the noisy aspirations of the air brake, and the busy *nok-nok-nok* of the compressor. It will take you eerily back to the days when we were all younger and the trolley was the favorite American car.

No. 34, shown here on the Branford trestle, is a single-truck open car, built in 1899 but restored to glistening condition.

Visitors on Sundays delight in riding on the old open cars.

Branford president E. J. Quinby, now only a weekend motorman, leans out the window of a special while awaiting a go-ahead.

For the not so fortunate hundreds, stacked three and four high and awaiting the acetylene torch, this is the end of the line. These cars in a San Pedro, Calif., yard were once the pride and joy of the Hollywood line.

ABOUT THE AUTHOR

The first trolley car that Frank Rowsome, Jr., rode was a Toonerville that lolloped along High Street, in Dedham, Massachusetts, in 1919. It bore him, alarmed but exhilarated, to kindergarten. Painted a shrill yellowish orange, it hissed like a snake when signaled to stop, and then unfolded a hidden doorstep in a fine spasm of ingenuity. Of all its mysteries, the most fascinating was probably the fare box, a glass-windowed contrivance that first caused coins to drop down a zigzag chute, and then swallowed them through a sneaky trap door, to disappear forever. A close second in enchantment was the brass sanding lever that was occasionally left behind by the motorman when he "changed ends" in the town square. Pressed firmly but furtively by a small child, this lever could produce mounds of sand on the track almost certainly large enough to discomfit the trolley that followed.

Graduating from Harvard in 1935, Mr. Rowsome wrote for and edited a number of magazines, mainly in semitechnical fields. He is presently the assistant managing editor of *Popular Science Monthly* and is chiefly concerned with testing and reporting on the newest automobiles. "The most horsepower-saturated vehicle out of Detroit," he notes glumly, "can't touch that High Street trolley for unadulterated willingness. It didn't go very fast, but it always *wanted* to go."

. . . and TECHNICAL EDITOR

Stephen D. Maguire, technical editor, has lived in New Jersey all his life, first in Jersey City and then in Belmar on the Jersey shore, where he has resided for the past forty years. He is a graduate of Rutgers University, Columbia University, and New York University Law School and now practices law in Asbury Park, New Jersey. He is also police magistrate of Belmar and South Belmar.

Interested in electric railways from his youth, he has collected material and souvenirs from trolley and interurban lines for most of his life. That collection is now one of the largest in existence, and it includes photographs, timetables, transfers, parts of trolleys, whistles, bells, headlights, marker lights, gongs, and destination signs, much of which can be seen at a permanent exhibit of trolley material in Lightner Museum of Hobbies in St. Augustine, Florida. He is also a member of many railroad and trolley-car historical groups and works in his spare time on the staff of *Railroad Magazine* as editor of the Electric Lines Department.